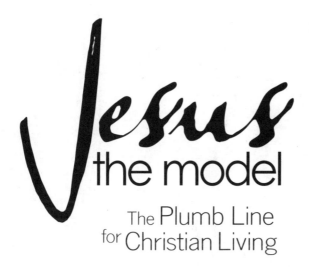

Jesus
the model

The Plumb Line
for Christian Living

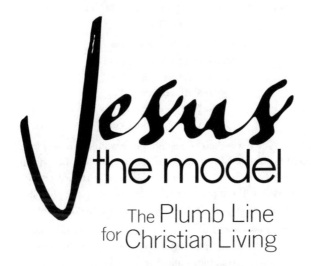

Jesus the model

The Plumb Line for Christian Living

JOY DAWSON

Charisma
HOUSE
A STRANG COMPANY

Library of Congress Cataloging-in-Publication Data:

Dawson, Joy.
  Jesus the model / Joy Dawson.
    p. cm.
  Includes bibliographical references and index.
  ISBN 978-1-59979-213-2 (trade paper)
  1. Jesus Christ--Example. I. Title.
  BT304.2.D39 2007
  232.9'04--dc22

                              2007015403

First edition

07 08 09 10 11 — 987654321
Printed in the United States of America

Started 11/5/07

Acknowledgments

My foremost debt of gratitude goes to God, who gave me the mandate to write on this subject and who has directed and enabled me throughout the process.

This is my seventh book. The biblical truths in this book about *Jesus the Model* and those in my first book, *Intimate Friendship With God: Through Understanding the Fear of the Lord*, have proven to be the most life-changing truths for me. I am deeply grateful to the Holy Spirit for revealing them to me as I diligently studied God's Word. I desperately needed them.

I am grateful to my beloved husband, Jim, for his availability to stop whatever he was doing and to patiently listen and comment on my writing efforts, as well as his many prayers for this project.

My gratitude also goes to Holly Holland, who has put this manuscript into the computer for me from my handwritten notes. She did a good job.

I am deeply indebted and very touched by the way my dear friend Pastor Jack Hayford has taken the time out of his demanding schedule to write such a meaningful, in-depth foreword to this book. I ask for a foreword, and he comes up with a literary masterpiece. I struggle to adequately convey the depth of my gratitude.

My deep appreciation also goes to my intercessor friends who faithfully prayed for me during the writing process and through the preparatory stages for publishing.

All the staff of Strang Communications with whom I interacted were so helpful—a delight to work with. My gratitude is very sincere.

Contents

Foreword

As you open this book, let me propose two thoughts:

First, about the writer: Joy Dawson never wastes words. That's why you will never waste time reading what she writes.

Second, about the subject: Jesus Christ is the Lord of *all* life. That's why you will never waste any of yours if you heed Him.

With those two maxims I urge you to read these pages, because you're being pointed to God's "original idea for life" as it has been displayed through His Son. As your guide, you have one of the most pointed and pungent friends you could hope to engage in assisting you toward seeing how that "idea" (actually, "ideal") can practically work and become effectively fruitful in your own life.

Years of observing the *life* of Joy Dawson, as well as the impact of her teaching on multitudes, have convinced me—you'll not do better or wiser than tuning in to her teaching. This petite, global Bible teacher and author makes more than an impression when she ministers. She leaves a permanent imprint. The beauty of this fact is this: when you are open to the Holy Spirit's grace, ministered through Joy's forthrightly direct and warmly inviting style, the engraved image left in your heart and mind is not of her—it's of Jesus!

When *He* is presented, as clearly and with purpose as in these pages, readers or listeners are led beyond the "religious" to the "relational"—from *words* to *the living Word*, from *facts* to *the Fulfiller*, from *information* to *transformation*, from *ideas* to *the Ideal*. The key to this full-dimensioned unfolding of both—Jesus as the ultimate *person* as the model and the ultimate *picture* of life, and Jesus' *power* as the Master who can unleash your and my ultimate *purpose* in life—is in the intensely practical way you'll find "His ways" presented here. You aren't left with theories or preachments, but you are given stories depicting principles that provide the same kind of "how to" that Jesus Himself intended us to grasp and apply.

So, there you are. Read those two thoughts again—the two I proposed at the beginning of this foreword. You'll be glad you spent the time to read this book, and even happier for what you discover in both the *beauty* and the power of Jesus—personally.

Christ in you, the hope of glory!

—JACK W. HAYFORD
PRESIDENT, INTERNATIONAL FOURSQUARE CHURCHES
CHANCELLOR, THE KING'S COLLEGE AND SEMINARY

Chapter One

JESUS THE MODEL
IN MINISTRY

The subject matter of this book is automatically exciting to me because it's all about the most fascinating Being in the universe, the Lord Jesus, the lover of our souls. Getting to know Him is being on a never-ending journey of wonder, amazement, awe, and intrigue. While His character is flawless and unchanging, His ways are at times past finding out. That means, mystery is part of who He is. He is like no other.

We must understand that the purpose of knowing Him is to be in intimate friendship with Him and to make Him known to others. But even more than that, it's that we may be conformed to

His image. Now, that's a deal. In fact, it's the biggest deal that we'll ever have going for us. Romans 8:28–29 says that God's primary purpose for our existence is that we may be conformed into the image of His Son. Wow, what a project for God! What a goal for us!

We hear Romans 8:28 quoted all the time: "All things work together for good to those who love God, to those who are the called according to His purpose." But many times we don't hear what immediately follows, which is what I have just referred to. This goal is what we should have in mind all the time.

The more I have studied Jesus' life, the more I am appalled at how far the body of Christ has moved away from the blueprint God has given us in His Word of how we are meant to live. If we don't think we need this message, it's a disclosure of how desperately we do.

Unbelief says, "I could never be enabled to live like Jesus did." Pride says, "I've got a better way," or, "I'm not willing to pay the price." Humility and faith respond, "I choose to live by the principles Jesus modeled for me as Son of man when He was here on Earth in the way He related to the Father." The greatest challenge. The ultimate fulfillment!

I can become like Him. There's only one person who can produce that miracle work in us. He's the precious Holy Spirit. In fact, He's the ultimate specialist! As we yield to Him daily, invite His total control, and obey His promptings, Christlikeness will emerge.

WHY JESUS CAME TO EARTH

The earthly life of Jesus Christ stands unique in human history as the pattern for all Christians. We cannot afford to glance at it. We have to study it thoroughly from God's Word, understand it, and then apply the same principles to our own lives.

We have to spend time consistently alone with Him, worshiping Him and listening to His voice. And above all else, obeying Him, instantly, joyfully, and wholly. The good news is, we do become like Him.

> But we all, with unveiled face, beholding as in a mirror the glory of the Lord, are being transformed into the same image from glory to glory, just as by the Spirit of the Lord.
> —2 CORINTHIANS 3:18

In Psalm 63:2 the psalmist says, "So I have looked for You in the sanctuary, to see to Your power and Your glory." There's no way that we can "behold" something and be casual. God doesn't reward casual inquiries about Himself, but He does reward diligent seekers.

5

JESUS THE MODEL

Jesus Christ relinquished all rights to function as Son of God to fulfill the purpose of being sent to Earth as Son of man. In order to do that, He laid aside His function of deity, but at the same time He retained His nature of deity.

JESUS CHRIST CAME TO EARTH FOR FIVE MAIN REASONS

We should be aware of these reasons and be able to quote them to ourselves and to others at any time.

1. He came to show us what the Father is like.

> The Son is the radiance of God's glory and
> the exact representation of his being.
> —HEBREWS 1:3, NIV

2. He came to die upon the cross to make atonement for the sins of the world.

This atoning work can be appropriated by those who repent of sin, invite Him to come into their lives as Savior, and make Him their Lord and Master.

3. He came to defeat the works of Satan.

> For this purpose the Son of God was mani-
> fested, that He might destroy the works of
> the devil.
> —1 JOHN 3:8

4. He came to show us how to live.

That's where we now kick in to the understanding of Jesus coming to lay aside His function of deity, retaining His nature of deity, to live as Son of man. Why? Because if He didn't, we wouldn't know how to live the Christlike life. We wouldn't know how to become like Him. "For to this you were called, because Christ also suffered for us, leaving us an example, that you should follow His steps" (1 Peter 2:21).

How in the world can we follow in His steps if we don't understand what He did and how He operated? That's what this teaching is all about. Because the Lord Jesus tells us to follow in His steps, that means He must be able to empower us to live like He lived. And we're going to see how He did. We may have many mentors, but only one model!   Jesus

First John 2:6 says, "He who says he abides in Him ought himself also to walk just as He walked." Multitudes of Christians have a huge boulder of unbelief in their hearts that needs to be removed through repentance. It's the boulder of unbelief that we can live like Jesus.

Before Lazarus came forth from the dead, what did Jesus say? "You roll away the stone, and then you'll see My glory." With repentance, we need to roll away the stone of unbelief in our hearts so that we can actually live like Jesus through the power of the Holy Spirit. Jesus would never tell us to do it if

7

He didn't have the power to enable us, because that would be unjust.

Let me explain how important it is that we understand the need to make Jesus our role model. We have many mentors in our life, and that's fine...it's all part of being discipled. As long as we understand that mentors never take the place of the one and only role model. If we model our lives on people who mentor us, that's idolatry. There's only one person who left heaven and came to Earth to show us how to live. It's the beautiful Son of God.

And in that context, I want to share with you something that happened to me when I was away on one of my many overseas ministry trips. I was speaking for a full week in a setting where there were a number of people being trained to be disciples. There was a strong leader, a man of God who was mentoring serious young people in their twenties. There were a number in the group who had leadership potential, but there was one young man who had more leadership potential than the others. I knew that. The leader knew that. God certainly knew that.

At 2:30 in the morning I was woken out of a deep sleep with an immediate awareness that God had woken me for a purpose. I was very alert. I sat up and said, "What is it, God? What do You want me to do? Pray? Speak to me. What is it?" And I heard clearly these words spoken into my spirit: "Go to the young

8

man in the training class who has the tremendous potential in leadership and say these words to him: 'Do not pattern your life on this earthly leader who is mentoring you. If you do, you will imitate his strengths and his weaknesses. Pattern your life only on the Lord Jesus Christ because He's your only model.'"

The next day I delivered the message. That young man listened. He heard. And today he is, and has been for many years, a strong leader over thousands of others. How very important that was.

5. He came to be our life.

It's one thing for Jesus to say, "Now follow in My steps and become like Me and do what I did." But we say, "How? We're just little finite creatures of the dust and He's the infinite God." Yes, but remember, He put aside His function of deity, retaining His nature of deity, living in absolute total dependence on the Father for everything. He came to show us how to live. And in essence He says, "OK, I know that you can't possibly live My life that I lived on Earth unless you understand that the fifth reason I came was to live My life in you so that I am the only explanation of what happens through you."

Paul understood this principle more than most; that's why he could testify in Colossians 1:27, "Christ in [me], the hope of glory," and in Galatians 2:20, "It is no longer I who live, but Christ lives in me." Paul could say that the only explanation of his life was the living Lord Jesus Christ whom he saw there on the Damascus road. We can't fully forgive others who hurt us unjustly. We can't fully love others who are unlovable—only Jesus' life in us makes those things possible through the person of the Holy Spirit.

I can say I have nothing going for me outside Him. I start each day of my life, and before I teach the Word of God, by saying, "Jesus, I have nothing going for me except Your life in me." Just as I come to consciousness each morning, I say, "Lord Jesus, You stand up in me and live Your life, Your way, through me this day." And then I say, "Think through my mind, look through my eyes, speak through my mouth, cause me to hear Your voice, love through my heart, touch through my hands, walk through my feet. Be the only explanation of what happens through me today." I tell Him I'm absolutely bankrupt and destitute unless He stands up and takes over in me, because I believe that without Him I can do nothing spiritual (John 15:5). It means that unless the Lord Jesus is in the driver's seat, in total control of my life, nothing spiritual is taking place, regardless of how much ministry activity in which I may be involved.

There's no other way that Jesus can be glorified, because Romans 7:18 says, "In me (that is, in my flesh) nothing good dwells." And Psalm 16, verse 2 says, "My goodness is nothing apart from

You." Do we realize this takes all the sweat out of Christian living?

Many years ago these truths revolutionized my whole life and particularly my prayer life. It simply means that before we minister to others in any way, we say, "I can't, but You can. I now lean on You, Jesus, so heavily that if You move I crash...with You. I trust You to take over through me. Thank You that You will."

The Lord Jesus' ministry falls into three main categories:

1. Teaching in the synagogue

2. Evangelizing out wherever the people were, meeting the needs of minds, bodies, souls, and spirits

3. Making disciples and training leaders

If we are called by God to be in positions of spiritual leadership, we need to check our lives to see if they match our role model. Of course, spiritual leadership requires a training process. There are no crash courses. But we should have a clear perspective of the ministry categories Jesus modeled for us.

There's a wonderful little book that I obtained called *The Life of Christ in Stereo*. I hope you can get it. It's very unique. The author has taken the trouble to take every significant aspect of Jesus' life from Matthew, Mark, Luke, and John, where a particular incident would be recorded in any one, two, three, or four of the Gospels, and combine the truths where each one has an aspect of Jesus in action at that point. In *The Life of Christ in Stereo*, they put it all together. Let me illustrate how Matthew 11:1, Luke 9:6, and Mark 6:12–13 are combined when we see it in stereo:

> And it came to pass that when Jesus had fin-
> ished commissioning His twelve disciples,
> He departed from there to teach and preach
> in their cities. And they went forth and made
> their way among the villages, announcing
> the glad news and healing everywhere. And
> they proclaimed that men must repent, and
> they cast out many demons and anointed
> with oil many persons who were sick and
> healed them.[1]

Isn't that beautiful? That's like a cameo of Jesus in ministry. That's what we're supposed to be doing, and if we're not, we're falling short of fulfilling the purpose of why Jesus came to show us how to live.

Chapter Two

CHARACTERISTICS OF JESUS' MINISTRY

This is so important. How can we become like others if we don't closely examine what they do and how they do it? I've learned more about people not by what they say, but how they live. How they react to God and people and circumstances. What the priorities of their lives are like.

Before I write any more, I want to state very clearly that there was never anything boring about Jesus' earthly ministry. It was always fresh, innovative, and humanly unpredictable; the unexpected was the normal. Does that sound like what usually happens when most Christians gather together? Hardly! What does that mean? What is God saying

13

to us, through pondering and facing up to those obvious differences between Jesus' way of ministering and ours in the body of Christ? It means that we desperately need to stop and ask God to reveal to us where and how our programs are not originating from waiting on Him, and then receive His specific directions for each time we come together as believers. If our services and gatherings are predictable, it means we're in a rut. And we're not operating on the principles Jesus modeled for us. Please keep those all-important facts in mind as we study the other strong characteristics of Jesus' ministry.

First, Jesus had single-mindedness, resoluteness, and intensity of purpose to accomplish the task that He had been given by the Father. Jesus said, "I have glorified You on the earth. I have finished the work which You have given Me to do" (John 17:4).

He wouldn't be diverted from fulfilling His purpose, at any cost. When Jesus said He was on His way to be crucified, Peter said, in effect, "That's not Your role! You're supposed to be the King coming in and taking over and freeing us all from the Roman rule." And Jesus said, "Get behind Me, Satan. You are an offense to Me, for you are not mindful of the things of God" (Matthew 16:21–23). And Jesus set His face as a flint to go to Calvary.

We need that kind of resolute determination to

fulfill our destinies. It's the same for all of us. It's Christlikeness. To know Him and to make Him known. If we're trying to make Him known and we aren't taking the time to know Him by studying His character and ways, and if He isn't the only explanation of our lives, do you know what we do? We give a distorted view of Him to others.

The second characteristic of Jesus in ministry, and by far the strongest, which tells us why He was so resolute to go the way of the cross, is humility. I would love that sentence to be written in caps, in bold, with underlining, and then have little stars around it. Why? Because it is the key to Jesus' life. And it has to become the key to ours. Humility is the way Jesus related to the Father. And there are five ways in which He did.

EVIDENCES OF JESUS' HUMILITY

1. His total submission to the Father

Luke 3:21–22 tells us that His first public act of submission to the Father was not in the miracles He performed. It was in His baptism by immersion. Immediately following that act of obedience, the dove came upon him, which was the sign of His being empowered by the Holy Spirit for public ministry. If we think that we can go out and minister and not follow Jesus in water baptism, and if we think that we don't need to be empowered by

15

the Holy Spirit for service, how proud can we get? These were Jesus' first public expressions of submission to the Father.

In Ephesians 5:18 we're commanded to be empowered by the Holy Spirit. The verb there for being empowered or filled is in the present continuous tense. In the original Greek it means, "be continuously being filled with the Holy Spirit." That's why I frequently ask God to fill me with His Spirit and also ask Him to show me if there is any undealt-with sin in my heart. Because God is a Holy Spirit, He doesn't fill dirty vessels. We've got to know if there's any undealt-with sin in our lives because sin separates us from intimacy with this beautiful Lord Jesus.

Do you know that conviction of sin is one of the greatest blessings that we can have? It helps us to get rid of the most destructive forces to our minds, bodies, souls, and spirits. Sin hinders Jesus' life being manifest through us to others. So we do ourselves the greatest favor by being convicted of it.

A couple of people have said to me, "Having heard you speak once, Joy, I thought I never wanted to come and hear you again because the message was so convicting." I have just smiled and said, "Well, that's your prerogative. That's fine. You're entitled to make your own choices." Those precious people had no understanding that God was doing them the greatest favor by convicting them of the

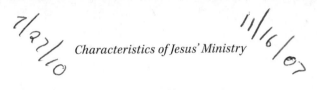
stuff that destroys us mentally, physically, emotionally, and spiritually.

I ardently pursue the Bible teachers and authors where the standard from God's Word will be raised up that I might have more understanding of what I'm to repent. I also seek out the ones who will challenge me to go deeper into the understanding of how I can be more Christlike.

Back to submission. In John 5:30, Jesus said, "I can of Myself do nothing. As I hear, I judge; and My judgment is righteous, because I do not seek My own will but the will of the Father who sent Me." He didn't come to live for Himself. He came to submit to the Father. He didn't have to think, "What will I do today?" He would be up early in the morning seeking the Father for His agenda for the next day (Mark 1:35).

I tell you honestly before God who knows my heart, I would be a nervous wreck if I thought I had to make the decisions for my life. I'm just a little weak, pea-sized, finite creature of the dust. I don't know what's best for me. Submission to Jesus is the greatest relief to me. I'm just a little sheep. He's the Great Shepherd. That's relief. Do yourself a favor, and surrender your whole life to Him.

2. *Jesus' humility in His dependence on the Father*

In John 5:19 we read, "Most assuredly, I say to you, the Son can do nothing of Himself, but what He sees the Father do; for whatever He does, the Son also does in like manner." When we look closely at that verse, we realize that Jesus never did a thing but what He saw the Father do and what He heard the Father say. That is why He had to spend so much time alone with Him. How much time do we spend, on an average, in our lifetime waiting on God?

For fifty years of my life I have been recording in diaries what God has been saying to us as Jim and I have sought Him diligently to know what we were to do in matters small or large. I've written down exactly what He said and the method He used to speak to us. The diaries are laced with these accounts because we don't know what's best for us. I don't know which invitations to teach the Word of God that I'm to accept and which ones I'm to decline. We don't know which is the best place to have a vacation. I don't always have the wisdom to know how to handle a difficult situation related to a relationship problem. But thank God, He does. And He's promised to give me that wisdom (James 1:5).

In John 8:28, Jesus said, "I do nothing of Myself; but as My Father taught Me, I speak these things." He also said in verse 38, "I speak what I have seen with My Father." He waited until He had seen and heard before He acted.

Many Christians give up after a number of minutes of waiting in God's presence for an answer about something. It's pathetic! That's why the Christian church is so relatively impotent and powerless and gives a distorted view of Jesus— because they themselves are the explanation of what is going on in their lives.

I am deeply convinced that the sin of presumption is one of the greatest sins in the body of Christ today. It holds back the fulfillment of God's eternal purposes on Earth and ultimately holds back the coming of the King. I'm deeply grieved about this sin, and therefore it is a major point of intercession in my life for the body of Christ worldwide to see it as God sees it.

Do you know what David said about this subject? We read about it in Psalm 19. David was a mighty man of God and an outstanding leader, as we know, but one of his greatest sins was the sin of presumption. As we study his life, we find that on several occasions there were devastating results from this sin. In Psalm 19, verse 13, David cries out, "Keep back Your servant also from presumptuous sins; let them not have dominion over me. Then I shall be blameless, and I shall be innocent of great transgression." In his later life he had the revelation of what the sin of presumption is from God's perspective. May we have the same revelation. Yes

Many times, because of the call of God on my life, I'm around spiritual leaders more than I am around other people, apart from my family. And out of that

19

lifetime of experience, I can say that this should be the cry of the hearts of spiritual leaders: "Keep me back from presumptuous sins. Then I shall be innocent and free from great transgression." I have seen the devastation that comes from the frequency of this sin.

So many times spiritual leaders come to me for counseling because this is a major part of the ministry God has given me. Time and time again when they share their problems and their perplexities with me, my first question is: "Did you seek the Lord until you knew He had answered you before you acted in that particular circumstance?" If I'm with a married couple, I ask if the wife had a story of divine guidance that was just as clear and strong as the husband. In the majority of cases, I have found that they were unable to answer me with an affirmative answer. The sin of presumption was at the root of the problems...debt, frustrations, lack of fulfillment, and much perplexity.

I remember a dear man of God who once came to me and said, "The six years I was on the staff of a very well-known church were the most miserable years in my Christian service. I have no understanding why."

I knew he didn't have a critical spirit. I knew the pastor of that church was an outstanding man of God. I knew the church was greatly used of God internationally. I said, "Did God speak to you in some distinct and definite way so that you had a story of 'God revealed His will to me, and this is how He did it' before you accepted the invitation to be on that staff?"

He said, "No."

I said, "What was the basis of your taking that major ministry responsibility?"

"The pastor asked me." The man didn't seek God for His answer.

There's a powerful exhortation in Psalm 62:5 that tells us what to do in times like that. "My soul, wait silently for God alone, for my expectation is from Him." Another one of my lifetime verses is Micah 7:7: "Therefore I will look to the LORD; I will wait for the God of my salvation; my God will hear me." Until we have the humility and faith to seek God for His answers on men's suggestions for our lives, we will hear God's disappointed heart cry:

> But My people would not heed My voice, and [they] would have none of Me. So I gave them over to their own stubborn heart, to walk in their own counsels. Oh, that My people would listen to Me, that [they] would walk in My ways!
>
> —PSALM 81:11–13

In Mark 1:35 we read that Jesus was up a long time before dawn, seeking the face of the Father.

The preceding day had been full of mighty miracles of healings and demonic deliverances. Jesus was teaching, both in the synagogues and out where the people were. In verse 33 it says, "The whole city was gathered together" and listening to Him. Regardless of all that spectacular ministry, Jesus never presumed upon what He was to do the next day or where He was to go. He was waiting on God for His orders and drawing on His fellowship with the Father for the strength to carry out the next day's assignment of teaching the multitudes and meeting the needs of the needy (verses 38–45).

Waiting on Father God was a way of life. There were no presumptions. It also demonstrates that Jesus had His priorities in the right order. He never made time with people a priority over time with the Father. What a model. What a challenge.

3. Jesus' humility in His obedience to the Father

In John 8:29 we read that Jesus said, "I always do those things that please Him." It's one thing to seek God and hear His voice to know what we're to do, but it's another thing as to whether we obey. Do you know what the biblical standard of obedience is? It has three parts to it. I hope you never forget this. Biblical obedience is instant obedience, not delayed. Delayed obedience is disobedience. Then biblical obedience is whole obedience, not partial obedience. Thirdly, it is obedience with joy and praise on our lips—no murmuring. So it is instant, whole, and joyful.

We can be positionally right, being in the will of God where He's told us to be, but conditionally wrong like the children of Israel. He said, "Go into the wilderness." They went into the wilderness. But what's the story of their behavior in it? Murmuring and unbelief. Positionally right, conditionally wrong.

Jesus never accepted praise from men.

Oh, I love this! Jesus said, "I do not receive honor [praise] from men" (John 5:41). Why? He couldn't and be logical, because the Father was the only explanation of what happened through the Son. And when you and I live this kind of life, being yielded to Him in submission, dependence, obedience, and faith, seeking to know His will until we hear from Him, He is the only explanation of what happens in and through us.

One alternative is for us to do our own thing living independently of Jesus' life in us, making our own decisions and relying on our own insights. That means we have to take the credit of what is happening through us. It also means there is zero spiritual content. The other alternative is to rely on the Lord Jesus for everything and then take the credit, which means "taking the glory to ourselves." Now that is obnoxious! In Proverbs 6:16 God lists seven things that are an abomination to Him. The top of the list is pride. So, the most abominable thing we can do is commit the sin of pride.

This kind of pride is totally illogical! If you've been convinced at the beginning of the day that you can't do anything spiritual yourself and that Jesus is the only one who can do it through you...who logically has to get the glory when He comes through? Let's use this muscle called our brain. It's just as simple an equation as two and two equals four. Who has to get the glory? Jesus. And it's also insane to touch the glory, because God says in Isaiah 42:8, "My glory I will not give to another." And in Malachi 2:1–2, there's a strong warning that says, "'And now, O priests, this commandment is for you. If you will not hear, and if you will not take it to heart, to give glory to My name,' says the LORD of hosts, 'I will send a curse upon you, and I will curse your blessings.'" I certainly don't want to be in that category.

Now would be a good time to take a reality check. Ask the Holy Spirit to reveal to you any area of your life where you may have knowingly or unwittingly failed to acknowledge to God and/or others that anything spiritual that has taken place in you and through you is solely attributable to the life of Jesus Christ in you.

Back to Jesus Christ. In John 14:10 He says, "Do you not believe that I am in the Father, and the

Father in Me? The words that I speak to you I do not speak on My own authority; but the Father who dwells in Me does the works." This beautiful Son of God knew no presumptions and no frustrations. Subsequently He lived a life that produced coordination and total fulfillment. How many frustrated Christians there are today, giving a distorted view of God's character to others. Think about it.

I have an answer for all this. In my tape catalog, there is a taped message listed that is one of the most important messages God has ever given me. It can be ordered through Youth With A Mission in Los Angeles, California. The title is "What to Do When Things Go Wrong." If you've never had a day in your life when things didn't go wrong, well, then we'll put you in a museum case and look at you and preserve you.

order

I can remember the day vividly (I'll never forget it as long as I live) when a nonstop series of surprising, illogical, unavoidable pressures were heaped on me, and it went on relentlessly.

In the middle of the day I dropped to my knees and prayed, "Lord, what is it You're trying to teach me?" Instantly He answered me, "I'm testing you to see how you will react under pressure." I had no idea back in those days the kind of pressure I was going to have to live under with an international traveling, teaching ministry—writing books, counseling people, and everything that goes with being a wife, mother, and grandmother and running a home, to name just some of the responsibilities.

I replied, "Oh, thanks very much. Then I can expect it to go on throughout the day, and I will receive Your grace." The relentless, unexpected pressures never lifted all day and evening. It was something else! But I knew what was happening. I knew, because I had asked God what I have come to call "the million-dollar question": "What are You trying to teach me?"

When there's a lack of coordination, or things are happening that we don't understand, and the circumstances are difficult, STOP, ask God that question, and keep on seeking Him until He answers you. He will start giving you answers. He gave me many answers because I made it a way of life. God loves to reward diligent seekers.

In the Second World War, the New Zealand Air Force had a saying for their airmen. It was, "Crash on regardless." Now, that may be a great slogan in a war situation, but it is not supposed to be the slogan for the Christians when things go wrong and they're not coordinating. Other Christians may add to the slogan by saying, "Well, just crash on and praise Him." Now that's better than not praising Him, but that's not the answer either.

Praising God, important as it is, is not necessarily the complete answer. We need to stop and wait on God. After praising God we should ask, "What is it You're trying to teach me?" As a result of most of a lifetime living that message, I have written a book called *Forever Ruined for the Ordinary: The Adventure of Hearing and Obeying God's Voice.* In it I share thirty-two reasons why God may delay an answer to our prayers. Now, how in the world did I learn that? I didn't get the material out of reading books. That whole book comes from the story of my life in walking with Jesus, wanting to be like Him, and waiting on Him as a way of life.

Instead of being frustrated, through waiting on God and persistently seeking His face, in time He will give us understanding. Remember, Jesus is our model. And in John 20:21 He says, "As the Father has sent Me, I also send you."

You may be thinking, "Well, Joy Dawson, it's all very well for you; you seem to hear God's voice easily, but I don't. How in the world can I hear God?" I understand. You may say, "I would do anything God told me to do if I only knew how to hear His voice." That's exactly what I said to God over fifty years ago in my life. And then I knelt down beside a bed in my little house in New Zealand (where we lived at that time) and said to God, "I don't know how to hear Your voice, but I do know that You've said 'My sheep hear My voice and I know them and they follow Me,' so I guess it's up to You to teach me."

Teach us Lord

JESUS THE MODEL

As I continued to seek Him for understanding with all my heart, He alone taught me. Never did I dream from that day, over fifty years ago, that I would teach people on every continent of the world how to hear God's voice and that I would also write a book titled *Forever Ruined for the Ordinary: The Adventure of Hearing and Obeying God's Voice*. In this book I share that there are twenty-four different ways that God communicates His mind and His heart to His children.

Because Jesus was always in humility through submission, dependence, seeking to know God's will until He heard, and total obedience, then He could always be in absolute faith.

We read in John 5:17 that Jesus said to them, "My Father has been working until now, and I have been working."

Jesus is relatively unimpressed with what we do in obedience to Him, whether it's to go to China and give ourselves to ministering to the underground church or it's to wash dishes or change a baby's diapers or raise the dead. None of these things is a big deal. The big deal is the One who gives the direction.

When we grasp that concept, then we obey joyfully, instantly, and wholly, because of who He is who speaks. Then we can say, "Oh, my Father's working, and I'm working, too."

STOP

Started again 11/16/0?

28

4. Jesus' humility was also expressed by His prayer life.

Why am I focusing so much teaching on Jesus' humility? Because that's the key to His life. And it's the key to yours and mine. Pride is our greatest sin. Humility is our greatest need!

In the book that I wrote titled *Intercession, Thrilling and Fulfilling*, I devoted the best and the last chapter to the prayer life of the Lord Jesus Christ. Nothing in print challenges my prayer life like what I discovered as I studied in detail every time where it is recorded that Jesus prayed. I'm always challenged out of my socks as I read about His prayer life, because that's what made His amazing life of ministry so effective.

Have you ever stopped to wonder why the disciples didn't say to Jesus, "Oh, Master, teach us to lead"? He was the greatest leader. Why didn't they say, "Teach us to teach"? He was the greatest teacher. Why didn't they say, "Teach us to administrate"? Let's face it: He had His act together! Why did they say to Him only, "Master, teach us to pray"? Because they saw that He never made priority of time more with man than He did over priority time with the Father. They started to get the connection between the power that came from His ministry and His prayer life. Do you know that your ministry and mine are only as powerful as our prayer life?

It's not more people laying hands on us and praying over us to be empowered by the Holy Spirit for ministry that is our greatest need. I'm not knocking any of that. That has its time and place. I'm not despising any of that at all.

But we would line up for an hour for someone to lay hands on us to have more power in prayer if we thought that was what would do it, but Jesus is waiting for us to discipline our lives and say, "I'm looking at Jesus' life, and I see that He took regular, quality time in His life to go aside with the Father for close fellowship with Him and to intercede for others."

What is prayer? Why is prayer so important, and how does prayer connect with humility? Prayer is inviting Jesus to come into every situation and change it from something natural to something supernatural so that He can get all the glory. It's terribly simple.

So, He can't get glory if we're not living like this as a way of life. Do we understand that prayer proves our dependence upon God? Oh, we can say we depend upon Him. That doesn't necessarily mean a thing! The proof that we really desperately need Him is that we're always asking Him to come in and change our circumstances from the natural to the supernatural. So what is the basis of all prayerlessness? Pride. Prayerlessness says, "I don't need You."

5. Jesus' humility was also manifest in His great emphasis on simplicity and the frequency with which He used children to illustrate this.

When I wrote my book *Influencing Children to Become World Changers*, I learned about the tremendous value that Jesus placed upon children and how He uniquely used them, not adults, to explain humility and simplicity. He acknowledged great faith in some adults, but when it came to simplicity and humility, He repeatedly said, "Look at children." Here are some of the scriptural references: Matthew 18:1–3; 19:13–15; Mark 9:33–37; Luke 9:46–48.

Jesus not only placed enormous value upon children, but He also had a deep concern for them. He passed the severest judgments on those people who caused children to stumble, with a warning against despising them.

In Matthew 18:6 we read, "Whoever causes one of these little ones who believe in Me to sin, it would be better for him if a millstone were hung around his neck, and he were drowned in the depth of the sea." How horrendous can the warning get?

Then in verse 10, Jesus warns against despising children. We can cause little ones to stumble by our wrong behavior, which gives them a distorted understanding of what God is like. Do we really get the weight of these implications?

JESUS THE MODEL

When Jim and I were bringing up our children, John and Jill, and the same with our six grand-children and our great-grandchildren, if we did or said anything that we were aware of that gave a distorted view of the character of God to them, we did our best to make restitution. We would say, "What we said or did there, we shouldn't have done, because we don't want you to think that God is like that. So we ask for your forgiveness." How impor-tant that was and is.

Unfortunately there were times when raising our children that we acted wrongly out of igno-rance. It was only looking back after several years that we realized we should have acted differently. As soon as we became aware of this, we apologized to them. Better late than never. Here's an example.

When our son John was sixteen years old, he was strongly influenced by the hippie revolution and wanted to have his hair long. That wasn't accept-able to us at that time. And as my husband Jim had always been John's barber, Jim insisted that John's hair be cut. This was a very painful thing emotion-ally for John. A few years later, when the Holy Spirit revealed to us that we were more concerned with our reputation related to John's appearance than how our decision was helping to create a wounded spirit in our teenager, we freely shared this with him and asked for his forgiveness.

On another occasion, I remember to my great

shame that I was breaking the speed limit (badly) when John (who was about twelve) spoke up from the backseat of the car, warning me that I was driving far too fast. Instead of slowing down, I gave back a comment that he was welcome to get out and walk if he wanted to. How gross! Many years later, when writing my first book, *Intimate Friendship With God: Through Understanding the Fear of the Lord*, I shared how my lack of the fear of God used to show up frequently by the way I would break the law by speeding. I shared that when I made an in-depth study from God's Word on the fear of the Lord, I discovered from Proverbs 8:13 that it meant to *hate* sin. That meant I had to have a hatred of breaking the law. It came, as I applied the fear of God to every area of my life.

Then the Holy Spirit reminded me of the above incident with John, many years previously. I repented deeply and asked John's forgiveness. It's never too late to humble ourselves. It pains me every time I think about that awful failure to represent Jesus to my child.

Jesus taught and lived humility as the key to having rest in our spirits and having the ability to cope under pressure of responsibilities.

In the Amplified Version, Matthew 11:28–30 reads like this: "Come to Me," said Jesus, "all you who labor and are heavy-laden and are overburdened, and I will cause you to rest. [I will ease,

and relieve and refresh your souls.] Take My yoke
upon you and learn of Me, for I am gentle (meek)
and humble (lowly) in heart, and you will find
rest (relief and ease and refreshing and recreation
and blessed quiet) for your souls. For My yoke is
wholesome (useful, good—not harsh, hard, sharp,
or pressing, but comfortable, gracious, and pleas-
ant), and My burden is light and easy to be borne."
Bottom line: How do we cope with pressure? Switch
into the humility gear.

That truth is possibly a new whole slant for
many on how we deal with stress. Think of all the
books that have been written on stress management. I know. I have a number of them in our home
library that have been sent to us by people who
have written on the subject.

And yet Jesus condenses the whole thing down,
typically of Him, into one simple statement. Jesus
has deep understanding of what stress is all about.
Have you ever stopped to think of the incredible
program that Jesus had, day after day orchestrated
by the Father? And yet we never, ever sense a hint
of any stress with the Son of God, regardless of the
enormous pressures and responsibilities.

Nothing is more stressful than crowds of people
pushing in and bearing in on us. It was so much
so that Jesus and His disciples, at times, didn't
even have time to eat their food. And yet Jesus was
always relaxed and in control and calm. How did

He do it? He gives the answer: "Take My yoke upon you and learn of Me." He didn't say, "Because I can give you ten points on how to cope with stress management." He says, "The secret of it is humility."

Are you overloaded? Say, "Jesus, show me my pride—the pride that I'm not depending upon You—the pride of presumption that I haven't waited to get Your directions. Or that I've perhaps taken on too much." Whatever it is, just ask the Lord to reveal where humility is needed to relieve the stress.

Chapter Three

JESUS WAS FORTHRIGHT AND TRANSPARENTLY OPEN

The third characteristic of Jesus in ministry is transparent openness and forthrightness in all His communications. Jesus' life on Earth was the embodiment of truth, holiness, and love. I greatly appreciate the directness of His personality that accompanied the way He manifested these characteristics.

Jesus never dodged an honest inquirer wanting truth about Himself. His life was an open book with absolutely nothing to hide. In fact, it cost Him His life to say that He was the Son of God.

JESUS THE MODEL

From the book *The Life of Christ in Stereo*, I'm going to share with you a time when Jesus was under cross-examination, from John 18:19–23.

> So the high priest questioned Jesus concerning His disciples and His teaching. Jesus answered him, "I spoke openly to the world, always I taught in the synagogues and in the temple with the Jews all assembled and I said nothing in secret. Why do you question Me? Question those who have heard Me as to what I said to them. Behold they know what I said."

That direct answer brought forth a rebuke from an officer, "How can you speak like that to the high priest?" Jesus again responded directly, "If I have spoken evil, bear witness of the evil; but if well, why do you strike Me?"[1] In other words, "My life is an open book."

I wonder if that is our testimony. Could we say, "I'm not afraid of being questioned because I'm only committed to speaking the truth"? That means I'm free. Jesus said, "You shall know the truth, and the truth shall make you free" (John 8:32). And if we're only committed to speaking truth, we don't have to think up an excuse. Wouldn't that be freedom to a lot of people! Are our lives such an open book that it wouldn't concern us what people asked us? That's how I have chosen to live.

We'll always cope with cross-examination if we have nothing to hide. If we are committed to speaking only 100 percent truth, we know we have the almighty God backing us, and we will always speak with authority and with wisdom. It was so with Stephen when he was confronted with much opposition: "And they were not able to resist the wisdom and the Spirit by which he spoke" (Acts 6:10).

Now, that doesn't mean that we have to answer everybody's questions, because Jesus didn't. Sometimes the wisest response is silence. It was so when Pilate asked Jesus why He was silent and didn't defend Himself when the chief priests accused Him of many things. It caused Pilate to marvel. (See Mark 15:3–5.)

God's Word also says, "Grace and truth came through Jesus Christ" (John 1:17). It's not enough just to speak the truth; it must be done graciously. And in Colossians 4:6 we're told our speech should always be with grace, seasoned with salt. That perfectly describes how Jesus spoke. There was nothing insipid about His words. Stop 11/16/0

Jesus could not tolerate hypocrisy in any form, and especially in spiritual leadership.

Nothing made Jesus Christ angrier than hypocrisy. He showed a holy hatred for it. In Acts 1:1 Luke

start 11/16/0

says, "The former account I made, O Theophilus, of all that Jesus began both to do [lived first] and teach." So we are not to teach something we haven't lived as a way of life. It's phony! Regardless of how fluent we may be in communicating the truth, there's no anointing. There's no authority. We can quote as many scriptures from the Bible and be speaking truth, but there's no authority if we haven't lived those truths. Hypocrisy is giving an impression that we are something we are not. People think that if we're speaking the truth and quoting it from the Word, then we're living it.

I want you to write something down that I hope you'll never, ever forget: *It's not sufficient to know the truth. We have to live the truth to be the truth. And it's only being the truth when teaching the truth that will cause God to release His authority on our teaching that will cause other lives to receive and act upon the truth.*

There was one thing that marked Jesus the model in His teaching ministry apart and distinct from all the other teachers in His day. The Bible says He taught with authority, which was different from the scribes. The scribes would teach the truths from the Old Testament but not live them; there was no authority. But the people noticed when this man Jesus spoke; He would be quoting the same Old Testament verses or truths, and there was authority. We never need to pray for liberty when speaking. We never need to pray for a gift of communication, necessarily. What we always need to pray for is authority when we speak. God will always answer that prayer if we are living the truths we're sharing and sent by God in His timing.

I remember being teamed with my dear friends Loren Cunningham, founder of Youth With A Mission, and Campbell McAlpine, a well-known Bible teacher from England. Both are wonderful men of God. The three of us had the responsibility of being teamed together in different countries, speaking for sometimes weeks at a time at spiritual leadership conferences. It was a great privilege for me to be teamed with them. We had a very unique, close relationship and learned so much from one another.

On one occasion, I was just about to speak at a conference session when I turned to my precious friend Campbell and said, "I feel so unprepared. I wish I'd had more time to prepare for this message."

He said, "Joy, is this message your life?"

I said, "Yes, every bit of it."

He said, "You are prepared." I remember the tremendous comfort that came to my spirit. Campbell understood this truth. The message was my life, and so I spoke with authority by the grace of God and through the enabling power of the Holy Spirit.

41

JESUS THE MODEL

Matthew 10:26 says, "For there is nothing covered that will not be revealed, and hidden that will not be known." Luke 12:2 says exactly the same thing. Those two verses are two of the most awesome verses that I know of in the Bible. I know what it is to tremble inside, in my spirit, and physically with my body when I think about their implications. "Nothing is covered that will not be revealed or hidden that will not be known." Do you believe that? If you do, it will alter the way you live. It will alter the way you think and speak.

In Matthew 23:27–28 we read:

> Woe to you, scribes and Pharisees, hypocrites! For you are like whitewashed tombs which indeed appear beautiful outwardly, but inside are full of dead men's bones and all uncleanness. Even so you also outwardly appear righteous to men, but inside you are full of hypocrisy and lawlessness.

Would we want our family relationships to be known to everybody? How we speak to one another as husband and wife? How we speak to our children? How we speak to our parents? How we speak to our brothers and sisters? How we speak to the people who work with us?

Would we want our thought life to be known? It has been. Jesus wrote with His finger on the

7\10\12

7/28/10

ground when a woman was caught in adultery and brought before Him, and the thought lives of the accusers were exposed. King Belshazzar had his life sentence written with the finger of God on a wall, and subsequently he died under the judgment of God.

Are we aware that at any time God can expose our thought lives as well as our words? If we do not repent of what is sin in our thoughts and our relationships down here on Earth, do you know where they're going to be exposed? At the judgment seat for all to hear. We do ourselves a favor to repent of anything that we don't want exposed openly, here or there. The Bible says that what we think is what we are. So we're not what other people think we are. We are what God knows us to be in our thought life.

How real are we? I will give an illustration here to show how we can be tested by God in relation to that question. It was the 1976 Olympic Games in Montreal. Eighteen hundred people had come from around the world under Youth With A Mission's leadership to witness in the streets of Montreal at the Olympic Games. It was the week beforehand where all the people who were going to witness had come together for a week's concentrated teaching under Youth With A Mission's leadership.

I was one of the Bible teachers, and one of the messages God had directed me to speak on was

STOP 11/16/07

7/10/12

11/17/07

10/28/10

"The Need to Be Empowered by the Holy Spirit for Effective Witnessing." It was the night before I was to give that message. I was in a trailer late at night with Loren and Darlene Cunningham, the founders of YWAM. The three of us were interceding for the next day's teaching sessions. We were also praying for many souls to be won for Christ at the outreach.

I was kneeling, praying for the lost to be saved and yearning for God's Spirit to reap the harvest of lost souls, when the conviction came from the Holy Spirit. I had a choice. I could be silent about what God was convicting me, or I could speak it out in front of my leaders. I chose to be real, and I spoke out these words: "O God, thank You for showing me my heart as You see it. I had no idea, Lord, until now, that the burden for lost souls that has marked my life is not what it used to be. You're showing me that I have allowed, not consciously, but subconsciously, all the weight of responsibility and time in preparation that goes with this Bible teaching ministry and while traveling around the world to become stronger than my life in personal evangelism. It's some months since I've led a soul to You. And whereas having times of effective witnessing to the lost was a way of life, I now see I have my priorities wrong." I repented at a deep level as I sobbed my heart out before the Lord in true brokenness. I didn't care what my leaders thought about me.

11/7/02

And then I said, "God, I'll do anything to have this burden for lost souls back on me, because obviously the reason why I haven't been witnessing as a way of life in the marketplace and wherever I have been in my travels is because I don't have the burden for their lostness that I used to have." *Help us Jesus*

I knew God had forgiven me, but in order to be real and to have my desperate prayer answered, I knew that I needed to seek God if there was anything more He required of me. I said, "I'll do anything. I'll do anything."

He quickly responded by saying, "You tell those eighteen hundred people tomorrow exactly what I've shown you here. Be open and broken in front of them." I immediately agreed.

I got up the next morning and told them exactly what God had said and added that I was so desperate for this burden for the lost to come back on my life, I would do anything God required of me to have it restored. I said, "Humbling myself before you all today is costly, but if that's what it takes, it's a small price to pay, because I won't let God go until He restores this needed priority in my life. I hope that I'll never be fooled into thinking a Bible teaching ministry is more important than my life in personal evangelism." And then, because of God's mercy and grace, I gave the message with authority.

Do you know what happened? As I looked back after that humbling that day, I realized God not only gave me back the burden I'd had before, but He also increased it—because humbling releases the power of the Holy Spirit. It's a spiritual law throughout God's Word. I have a whole message solely on that subject. How desperate are we to be like Jesus, where reaching the lost was a way of life with Him?

After I had spoken at a church about the importance of being real, the pastor who had invited me said, "Joy, I totally understand what you are saying about this reality thing. One Sunday I got up in my church to speak on 1 Corinthians 13, the love chapter. I knew that God had directed me to read from that portion of Scripture. I presumed I was to speak from it and had prepared to do so. I started reading, and when I came to the verse that says, 'Love is patient and kind,' the Holy Spirit said to me, 'You're often impatient with your wife.'" The pastor continued, "I had a choice at that moment. I could have responded silently, 'Yes, God, I'll repent later,' and continued to read and then give the message. Or I had the opportunity to be more real than that."

I said, "What did you do?"

He said, "I just looked at the audience and said, 'I often confess impatience to my wife. It's not that I'm insensitive to this failure in my life. But I'm

46

tired of doing that. I need a change of heart and life concerning this sin.'"

He continued, "I turned around. I never said another word to the audience. I knelt in front of the big chair [the one reserved for the pastor] and buried my head in it and sobbed my heart out as I wrestled with God, saying, 'I will not let You go until You bring me to deep repentance.'"

I understood what my pastor friend was wrestling with God for. I've had to do the same thing when God has convicted me of sin. Repentance is a change of mind, a change of heart, and a change of life toward sin. All he had previously done was to change his mind.

The pastor told me that he continued to seek the face of God and said "I'm not going to leave You in this place until You meet me." He explained, "Joy, I was there for about thirty minutes, sobbing my heart out. When I knew that God had met me and my heart was changed and I had the fear of God upon me in relation to this sin (which is to hate it), I thought to myself, 'Well, the church will have emptied out, but so what? I'm changed.'" Then he said, "When I got off my knees, I couldn't see anyone in their seats…because they were all prostrate on the floor, sobbing their hearts out.

"Nobody had left. The Spirit of God had sovereignly moved into the church, brought the congregation under deep conviction of sin, and I hadn't had to preach one word. I just needed to be real. That Sunday we had the deepest move of God's Spirit. The people were broken, weeping, and getting right with God. I was changed, and so were they. All glory to the Lord." I think the point is made.

There's another important truth that runs parallel with what has just been shared. Jesus said, "Woe to the world because of offenses! For offenses must come, but woe to that man by whom the offense comes" (Matthew 18:7).

Jesus is teaching here that there is accountability to God and required repentance on each person who is a cause of tempting or provoking another person to sin. We can be doing just that by repeated speech patterns that tempt another person to frequent impatience.

JESUS HAD GREAT COMPASSION FOR HUMAN NEED AND SUFFERING

Jesus' compassion was vividly demonstrated by the enormous emphasis He placed upon healing the sick and releasing people from tormenting evil spirits. It was not only an integral part of His methods in evangelism but also what He taught His disciples to do (Matthew 10:8). Jesus' miraculous feeding of the thousands, on the recorded occasions in the Gospels, also demonstrates His compassion and concern for human need.

I know a dynamic evangelist who for years had been used of God to bring many thousands of unconverted people into Christ's kingdom. Then God sent someone to him who asked him to seek God about adding a new dimension to his gospel preaching. It was simply to operate on the same principles Jesus did—which was to overtly present the Lord Jesus as the healer of the body as well as the Savior of the soul. In other words, make Jesus his model as an evangelist. The Holy Spirit confirmed to him that this was the word of the Lord, and in humility he received it.

From the first time he applied this additional aspect to his gospel preaching, God confirmed His Word with demonstrations of the miraculous. And it has relentlessly continued. As a result, many more unconverted people attend his outreaches, and many more are giving their lives to Christ. The key was making Jesus his model.

I know of other preachers who made the same commitment and faithfully presented the truth of Jesus forgiving all our sins and healing all our diseases (Psalm 103:3). But they were greatly tested. It was months before the breakthrough came in the displays of the miraculous. But they never gave up presenting the gospel as Jesus did, and in time, He greatly rewarded their obedience and faith.

Start
11/17/07

7/10/12

Jesus had a burdened heart for people, not just a head full of truth. Matthew 9:36 says, "When He saw the multitudes, He was moved with compassion for them, because they were weary and scattered, like sheep having no shepherd."

I have a whole message that is available from my tape catalog on "What It Means to Have a Burdened Heart for the Lost." What does that involve? All I'm going to give here is the basic outline, without any of the teaching or the illustrations.

A person with a burdened heart for the lost is filled with the love of God for them. A burdened heart for the lost intercedes for them. A burdened heart for the lost weeps for them. A burdened heart for the lost gets personally involved in the lives of the lost. A burdened heart for the lost is willing to lay down their life if necessary for them.

This message is one of the most powerful messages that I've given. There's also a sequel to that message, titled, "How Do You Get a Burdened Heart for the Lost?" And that's in my catalog. Both can be ordered from Youth With A Mission, 11141 Osborne Street, Lake View Terrace, California 91342, USA.

What is our reaction to the grotesque? We may say, "I've got compassion for hurting people. I'll go up to anybody; it doesn't matter what their condition." I'll tell you when God tested me on that one. I was in Calcutta, India, on one of the several teaching ministry trips that I've been on in that country.

I was visiting Mother Teresa's ministry. I was very slowly walking through her ministry compound, talking to the nuns and to the needy people, when it happened. Suddenly I saw a piece of humanity in a sitting position on the bare floor. I had no idea whether it was a male or a female. There were no distinguishing signs. I could see no legs. The head, which was completely shaved, was gyrating in all directions. And out of the mouth were sounds like the barking of a dog. I presumed that was a sign of demon possession.

I have said and believed that "love's arms hate to be empty." I have believed that Jesus would embrace any human being in His arms under any condition when prompted by His Father, and I am committed to being like Jesus. The Bible says, "Perfect love casts out fear" (1 John 4:18). I had no idea what the reaction would be as I walked alone toward this individual. But I did so, without any fear, with God's love filling my heart for this desperately needy soul.

I leaned over and gently embraced the person. Then I kissed the person on both cheeks; I kept kissing the top of the head while quietly saying, "Jesus loves you. Jesus loves you. I love you." As I gently kept repeating these words, all the barking stopped, the head stopped gyrating, and stillness with complete peace came over that precious individual. I didn't know whether he or she understood the language I was speaking. But everyone knows the language of God's pure love. And I knew the Holy Spirit had ministered that language through me to that person. The result was comfort, calmness, and release from torment. The pure, fervent love of God is the strongest force in the universe. And satanic forces have no counterfeit for it.

7/10/12

Chapter Four

Jesus' Teaching
Ministry

11/17/07

I have purposely reduced Jesus' teaching ministry to three simple concepts because I believe
they are the "bottom line" basics, which can be
explained, understood, memorized, and applied by
children as well as adults. I want these three concepts to so burn in your spirit that you'll never forget
them and that you'll repeat them constantly, so that
you can (as I do) measure your life by them.

Jesus' First Message Was "Repent"

"From that time Jesus began to preach and
to say, 'Repent, for the kingdom of heaven is at

11/17/07

7/10/12

hand'" (Matthew 4:17). As I've already written, but it is worth repeating, *confession* is the first step toward repentance. It is a change of mind toward the sin. I agree with God's spirit of conviction and acknowledge it.

Now we need *a change of heart*. I want to see this sin as God sees it, feel about it as He does. I can only repent to that level. I ask for that revelation with intense desire and believe He will grant that request. We can't have a change of heart until we see it as God sees it.

In my life I've had to, at times, wrestle with God as Jacob did and tell Him, "I won't let You go. I won't get up from my knees until You give me a revelation of my heart as You see it." It's been some of the most life-changing, liberating experiences of my life. We don't go back to those sins once we've seen them as God sees them. We weep intensely with deep brokenness before God. It's devastating but wonderful, because we know that only the oncoming of the Holy Spirit could produce this spiritual phenomenon.

The third aspect of repentance is *a change of life*. I ask for the fear of God, which is to hate the sin I once loved. That's why I chose it in the first place. There are two reasons why we sin. One, we choose to. Second, because we have a love for it. Proverbs 8:13 says, "The fear of the Lord is to hate evil [sin]." So the more we ask for the fear of Lord and keep receiving it by faith, the more God will give it to us. You may say, "How will I know when the fear of the Lord is operating in my life?" By your new attitude toward that sin. Instead of being tempted by it, you now hate it. We don't do the things we hate, unless we are forced to by a higher authority.

I've written a book on this subject titled *Intimate Friendship With God: Through Understanding the Fear of the Lord*. There are sixteen chapters on how the fear of the Lord affects every part of our lives. It is the most life-changing subject I've ever studied, parallel to this series on the life of the Lord Jesus.

After John the Baptist was arrested, Jesus continued to teach openly on repentance. In Mark 1:15 we read, "The time is fulfilled, and the kingdom of God is at hand. Repent and believe in the gospel." Later, in Mark 6:12, again we find Jesus telling His twelve disciples to teach the message of repentance: "They went out and preached that people should repent." Luke alone records another ten references to the Lord's teaching on repentance.

To add to the significance and importance that Jesus gave to this teaching, we find Him declaring it again in Luke 24:7. The setting was in the last discourse that Jesus had with His disciples before He went up to heaven. He said plainly that the whole purpose of His death and resurrection was that repentance and remission of sins should be preached in His name to all nations.

How long has it been since you have heard a whole message on repentance? How long has it been, if you're a spiritual leader or a Bible teacher, since you taught on repentance? Do you understand the extent of the implications of biblical repentance? Is it a way of life with you? It was so important to Jesus that it was His first message.

Why was the subject of repentance Jesus' first, middle, and final message? I believe it's because undealt-with sin hinders our intimate friendship with God, which hinders our goal of being conformed into Christ's image, which hinders the fulfillment of our destinies.

"Follow Me"

The second main message was terribly simple. It was two words: "Follow Me." These words mean, "Watch Me, listen to Me, learn from Me, understand Me, and do what I did in the power of the Holy Spirit." In John 8:12, we read: "Then Jesus spoke to them again, saying, 'I am the light of the world. He who follows Me shall not walk in darkness, but have the light of life.'" Following Jesus is seeking Him, listening to Him, studying Him, being alone with Him, worshiping Him, loving Him, obeying

Him, depending upon Him, and making Him the only explanation of our lives.

What does it mean to follow Him? It means to live in obedience. To what? To revealed truth and the promptings of the Holy Spirit in the smallest things. You can ask my children, my husband, and my grandchildren. All of my closest family members will tell you that the secret of my life as a Christian is contained in this one sentence: doing the next little thing God tells me to do. That's not complicated. All the greatest doors of opportunity that God has given me to make Him known internationally, and they have been many, have come through constant obedience to revealed truth and the promptings of the Holy Spirit, no matter how small.

"GO AND TELL"

Jesus' last message was, "Go into every nation and tell them everything I have told you." (See Matthew 28:19–20.)

What was the continuing message throughout His ministry? Repent. What was His second message? "Follow Me and obey Me." What was His third message? "Go and tell them about Me." So simple! How have we ever made it so complicated? Through pride and unbelief.

I'm going to close this chapter with a powerful testimony that I heard Dr. Jack Hayford give at a

11/17/07

7/10/12

meeting I attended. He's one of the most influential pastors in the world today. He's traveled the world, and still does, and has written many books. He said that as a young man in his early days of attending Bible college, not knowing what his life's ministry would be, he attended a missions convention.

The speaker explained that to every disciple of the Lord Jesus, He has given a command in Matthew 28:18-19: "All authority has been given to Me in heaven and on earth. Go therefore and make disciples of all nations, baptizing them in the name of the Father and of the Son and of the Holy Spirit."

Jack Hayford said, "I knew at that point that I had never responded to that command. I pondered the implications of what it could mean. For the first time in my life as a young man preparing for ministry, I weighed the consequences of this response to Jesus. It could mean that I would spend the rest of my life in some foreign country, away from my family and friends and in anything but comfortable conditions. I'd perhaps have to learn another language."

He continued, "I did not respond quickly. Finally, slowly but very deliberately, I walked from the back of that missions convention meeting to the front and said, 'Jesus, I respond by saying yes to You. I'm willing to be sent by You, anywhere, under any conditions, at any time.'"

He went on to explain that it was only after that commitment that the Holy Spirit very clearly revealed to him, at a later time, that his life's ministry was to be a pastor in his own country of America. He didn't know then that God would be sending him as a pastor from that country to many nations of the world to speak to pastors all over the world and that pastors from all over the world would come to hear him teach God's truths from His Word.

Finally, he said, "And you will never know what your life's ministry is until you have responded as seriously as I did to the Great Commission that day." That's the point I want to emphasize! It makes sense, doesn't it? Why should God give us directions for our life's calling if we haven't been obedient to this pivotal command?

OK. Back to Jesus. I love the bracelet that people wear with the words "What would Jesus do?" written on it. That's really getting to the heart of how we should act and react in every given situation. And when it comes to evaluating the weight of what we're sharing as Bible teachers, we should be asking, "What did Jesus teach?"

Jesus said to His close friends, "Do you also want to go away?" I love Peter's answer, and it's my answer today. "Lord, to whom shall we go? You have the words of eternal life" (John 6:67–38). Jesus

11/17/07

7/10/12

had just previously said, "The words that I speak to you are spirit, and they are life" (verse 63).

We do ourselves the greatest favor by meditating on everything Jesus said and modeling our lives and teaching accordingly, because, "No man ever spoke like this Man!" (John 7:46).

We then do ourselves an equal favor by allowing the Holy Spirit to shape us into the image of this exquisitely beautiful, wonderful, fabulous, precious, infinitely wise, awesomely holy, unswervingly faithful, strong-as-a-lion, meek-as-a-lamb, and totally just Being. He is the only One to whom we will give an account at the judgment seat. On that awesome occasion, God the Father will ask, "What did you do with what Jesus said? Did you make it your goal to be like Him?" My prayer is that everyone reading these words will not be ashamed when these questions are asked.

Stop

APPLICATION OF THIS TEACHING

1. If you know God has spoken to you personally from this teaching, thank Him and praise Him. That's an act of humility.

2. Mark the areas where you come short of the standard of Christ's life, related to the following:

7/10/12

- *Single-mindedness and intensity of purpose to accomplish the task given Him by the Father.* Are you easily distracted from this pursuit personally?

- *Humility in the way He related to the Father*
    (a) Absolute submission: Can you honestly say, "The answer will always be yes to anything the Lord asks me to do"?
    (b) Absolute dependence: seeking to know the Father's direction in all things. Jesus said, "It is the Father living in Me who is doing His work." Are you so dependent on the Holy Spirit at all times that you can say, "Without Him I can do nothing (of spiritual significance)"?
    (c) Absolute obedience: not partial, delayed, or with murmuring.
    (d) And faith at all times that the Father is working, no unbelief.

- *Humility, emphasized by His many references to childlikeness*

7/10/12

- *Humility, the key to coping with pressure of responsibilities*

3. Jesus was transparent in all communications; He exhibited 100 percent honesty at all times.

4. Jesus was devoid of all hypocrisy and showed hatred of it.

5. Jesus had great compassion for human need and had involvement to meet it.

6. Jesus had right priorities, as shown by His consistent prayer life.

7. What was the distinguishing mark of Jesus' teaching ministry?

8. What were the three main emphases of Christ's teaching?

9. Do the following three things, as a way of life, characterize your responses to Jesus' teaching?

- Repentance of all known sin, including making restitution to others

7/10/12

- Following Him by studying His life, listening to His voice, learning from Him, obeying Him, and worshiping Him as a way of life

- Responding to His command to go into all the world with the good news of the gospel—short term or long term as He directs—and witnessing to the lost as a way of life

10. Is it your life's goal to be more like Jesus as you submit to the control of the Holy Spirit? Does your lifestyle prove it?

11. Finally, acknowledge to someone else the areas of your life where you have determined to change in order to fulfill your destiny of Christlikeness. (See Romans 8:28.) Pride is our greatest enemy. Humility is our greatest need. Are you able to give Scripture references for the above teaching?

Chapter Five

JESUS THE MODEL IN FRIENDSHIP

One of the most popular hymns that is sung by millions of God's children is, "What a Friend We Have in Jesus." We receive comfort every time we sing it. We're meant to. One of the main purposes for which we were created is that we may experience an intimate relationship with our wonderful Savior, the Lord Jesus.

The good news is that He longs for us to experience Him as friend at the deepest possible level. The sad news is that so many don't realize this fulfillment. Could it be that we haven't taken the time to study the aspect of Jesus as a friend from God's

7/10/12

Word? The more I have, the more fascinated I have become with this amazing person.

To understand Him as the ultimate spiritual leader and at the same time the perfect friend, we have to go back to the basics. By coming to Earth and functioning as the Son of man, Jesus never lost sight of the fact that by nature and relationship, He was the Son of God. Therefore, His first allegiance and responsibility was to His Father God. The strong priority of that vertical relationship was the primary cause of the strength He gave to His horizontal relationships. We can never give any greater strength to an earthly relationship than the strength and depth of our relationship to the Godhead. Jesus, the model friend on Earth, could say, "I always do those things that please Him [the Father]" (John 8:29).

This truth was evident early in His life when He was a boy. Joseph and Mary finally discovered Jesus sitting in the temple, talking to and questioning the religious leaders, after having searched for Him for days. His response to their inquiry as to why He had caused such anxiety was simply, "Why did you seek Me? Did you not know that I must be about My Father's business?" (Luke 2:49).

Paul understood the concept that just as Jesus' primary focus relationally was toward the Father, so our primary focus relationally must be on Jesus. In 1 Corinthians 7:23 we read, "You were bought at a price; do not become slaves of men." Then verse 35 says we are to live in "undivided devotion to the Lord" (NIV).

All our relationships will suffer unless we make and keep the Lord Jesus as our priority in friendship. My book *Intimate Friendship With God* makes this very clear. God-given friendships have divine purpose. One purpose is to link ministries together for the extension of God's kingdom. Another purpose is to meet needs in each other. The ultimate illustration of this point was when Jesus expressed His desperate need in the Garden of Gethsemane to Peter, James, and John: "My soul is exceedingly sorrowful, even to death. Stay here and watch" (Mark 14:34). And then in verse 37, "Could you not watch one hour?" Jesus' closest men friends failed Him at His time of desperate need by choosing sleep. God the Father also gave the Lord Jesus three close women friends when He was on Earth. I believe they were His mother Mary, Mary of Bethany, and Mary Magdalene. All three displayed unusual faithful, intense devotion to their Master. As Son of man, Jesus needed close friends—both men and women. This need was met by the Father. Jesus was not an isolated recluse, withdrawn from society.

Therefore we too can expect God to give us the close friendships of His choosing in our lifetime.

7\10\12

How do we get them? I am giving you the following seven ways, all biblical principles:

- Have the humility of seeing our desperate need of having friends.

- Ask God to bring friends into our lives and believe that He will in His time.

- Be obedient to revealed truth and the promptings of the Holy Spirit as a way of life.

- Be transparently honest with friends when He does bring them, and acknowledge our need to learn from them.

- Welcome their loving corrections when they are confirmed by the Holy Spirit and are in line with the principles in God's Word.

- Be a faithful, loyal, loving, caring, and committed friend to them.

- Never disclose things they have shared in confidence.

Now Let's Focus on Jesus' Life

7/10/12

The closer we look at Him as the model friend, the more we find His life is marked with purity and naturalness. In all circumstances, Jesus is completely free from embarrassment or awkwardness, self-consciousness or tension. After all, He was, and is, the embodiment of TRUTH.

God's Word tells us that truth sets us free—free to be transparent, with nothing to hide; free to quickly "rejoice with those who rejoice, and weep with those who weep" (Romans 12:15).

There are three important things that we need to understand regarding the friendships God the Father gave Jesus as Son of man:

1. They were in categories.

2. There were degrees of closeness in those categories.

3. They were with both sexes.

Let's observe the category of those He was teaching and training as disciples and their degrees of closeness to Him.

■   There were the seventy that He sent out to evangelize two by two.

7/10/12

- There were the twelve apostles.

- There were Peter, James, and John.

- There was John—the disciple whom Jesus loved.

Now let's look at Jesus' women friends in the same way.

- There were the women mentioned in Luke 8:2–3 who were His and His disciples' financial supporters— three in particular, and "many others who provided for Him from their substance" (Luke 8:3).

- There were the women who were concerned for Jesus' suffering and who tried to comfort Him when He was on His way to Calvary. "And many women who followed Jesus from Galilee, ministering to Him, were there looking on from afar, among whom were Mary Magdalene, Mary the mother of James and Joses, and the mother of Zebedee's sons" (Matthew 27:55–56).

7|10|/2

Out of that category came Mary Magdalene and Mary the mother of Jesus. They were the last at the cross when everyone else had gone, and then they waited and saw Joseph of Arimathea put Jesus in the tomb. They also went with Salome very early in the morning to anoint Jesus, but found the tomb empty. The intense devotion to Jesus is then uniquely manifest by Mary Magdalene, as we read in John 20 that she alone ran from the tomb and told Peter and John that it was empty and that she didn't know what had happened to His body. Her singular devotion showed up again when, after those disciples had seen the empty tomb and returned to their homes, she went back to the tomb alone, weeping... still searching for the love of her life, Jesus.

No wonder she was rewarded by being the first person on Planet Earth to engage in friendship with the risen Christ—and then to be the first person to proclaim the message of His resurrection to mankind.

How terribly special Mary Magdalene must have been to the Lord Jesus at that point and from that point in time. By the way, it amazes me that this precious woman is constantly referred to as having been a prostitute, whereas there is not a single reference in the Bible to support this fallacy.

Now we see from Jesus' friendship with Martha, Mary, and Lazarus of Bethany a close degree of friendship in the family category. Yet Mary stands out as having the most intimate relationship with Jesus within that circle. She alone chose to sit at His feet, listening intently to His teaching. And in John 12:3 she is described as anointing Jesus' feet with expensive ointment and wiping His feet with her hair. This lavish expression of intense devotion was rewarded with strong affirmation from the Son of God. We notice that this closeness in relationship was totally devoid of any sexual connotation. What models they are for us as we embrace the truth that with the fear of God as our covering, godliness and naturalness go hand in hand.

It is interesting to see in the Scriptures another category of relationships Jesus had. It was with those to whom He ministered personally. For example, when He went to Zacchaeus, the tax collector's house; when He revealed Himself as the Messiah to the Samaritan woman at the well; the time He spent with Nicodemus, the teacher of the law; and many more.

Because God the Father gave all these categories of friendships, with their varying degrees of closeness to His Son when He was on Earth, we can expect that our Father God has earthly friendships planned and prepared for us.

We will only be able to receive and enjoy those precious and needed gifts to the degree that we make sure that we are the right person, in the right place, at the right time, saying and doing the right things. In other words, we are pursuing the principles by which Jesus lived when He was on Earth.

CHARACTERISTICS OF JESUS AS A FRIEND

Have you observed that He was the friendliest possible person? Proverbs 18:24 says, "A man who has friends must himself be friendly." Jesus' most wonderful characteristic was His unconditional love. True love must be based in humility. In fact, we're only as loving as we're humble. Unconditional love doesn't depend on the other person's righteousness or unrighteousness, their repentance toward you or lack of it, their reciprocation of love to you or failure to give it, or any reward or gratitude for your love. This kind of love is entirely supernatural. It is described in John 15:12 when Jesus said, "This is My commandment, that you love one another as I have loved you." It is only attainable by the deep working of the Holy Spirit in our lives: "The love of God has been poured out in our hearts by the Holy Spirit who was given to us" (Romans 5:5).

Jesus manifest this unconditional love in the way He freely forgave everyone who wronged Him. It was only because He was the forgiving friend as a way of life that He could pray the ultimate prayer of forgiveness for those who had crucified Him:

"Father, forgive them, for they do not know what they do" (Luke 23:34).

In the Garden of Gethsemane Jesus faced the traumatic agony of what it would mean to become sin for mankind by His atoning death on the cross and, at the same time, to be separated from the Father with whom He has been in unclouded communion before time began. Those implications are far beyond our finite comprehension. We just know that He sweat blood from the pores of His precious skin!

Straight after *that*, Jesus faced His follower Judas heading up a large crowd of soldiers together with officers from the chief priests, scribes, and Pharisees coming with swords and clubs. Judas identified Jesus by kissing Him, saying, "Greetings, Rabbi." Jesus' incredible response was, "*Friend*, why have you come?" (Matthew 26:49–50, emphasis added). "Judas, are you betraying the Son of man with a kiss?" In the face of horrible betrayal and nauseating hypocrisy by a false display of affection, Jesus identifies Himself in friendship with Judas, calling him FRIEND.

The key to this magnificent display of amazing grace is that Jesus dealt with the temptation to be resentful and bitter toward Judas years before these events. Jesus chose to forgive him when the Father had revealed to His Son that Judas would betray Him: "'But there are some of you who do not believe.' For Jesus knew from the beginning who they were who did not believe, and who would betray Him" (John 6:64).

We can only be hurt to the extent that we love. Therefore, the more we love, the more we need to know how to forgive. Jesus is the friend who loves the most. He gets hurt the most and amazingly forgives the most. When we get hurt, we instinctively want to withdraw from the person who hurt us. Pride says, "I don't need you." Humility says, "I do need you." God the Father gave Judas to Jesus as a close ministry partner, and Jesus never withdrew from that relationship. He gave His life for Judas' redemption. Judas withdrew from his friendship commitment to Jesus. It was the cause of Judas' death.

After Peter had vehemently denied his Master three times, including with oaths and curses, we read in Luke 22:61–62, "And the Lord turned and looked at Peter.... So Peter went out and wept bitterly." One look into Jesus' eyes instantly melted Peter into deep repentance. How could this be? Only because those eyes that burn with the fire of God's white-hot holiness also burn with the fire of God's unfathomable, all-encompassing, unconditional, loving forgiveness...which includes the worst sins ever committed by mankind.

Jesus, the perfect friend, understood how hard it would be for Peter to believe that He would really

12/12

forgive him and for Peter to be able to forgive himself. That's why the Godhead dispatched a special angel from headquarters heaven to be at the empty tomb and give this startling message to the women, "Do not be alarmed. You seek Jesus of Nazareth, who was crucified. He is risen! He is not here....But go, tell His disciples—*and Peter*—that He is going before you into Galilee" (Mark 16:6–7, emphasis added).

Then, in Luke 24:34, there is another singularly significant reference to Peter, related to Jesus revealing Himself to the one who so badly needed to have assurance of the Master's forgiveness: "The Lord is risen indeed, and has appeared to *Simon* [before the other men disciples]!" (emphasis added).

God's mercy is always extended to a truly repentant heart.

All the disciples were going to need to believe that truth, because Jesus had to forgive them for forsaking Him at His trial and for not believing Him when He had repeatedly told them He would rise again from the dead. The sin of unbelief not only grieves God's heart, but it also hurts Him deeply.

This truth was emphasized to me one time when my husband, Jim, and I were interceding for America, where we have lived since 1971. We were asking God to share with us, as His friends, where He was hurting the most in relation to our nation. He immediately replied by speaking into our spirits,

"They have discarded My Word, the Bible, as being irrelevant. They have rejected Me."

We waited in God's presence, felt and expressed some of His grief, and vicariously asked for His forgiveness for our nation. As we continued to seek Him, He spoke again, "Those who believe the Bible is My Word so often don't read it." More shared grief. More asking for forgiveness. We pursued our beloved friend Jesus for more understanding of what was causing Him pain. Lastly, He said, "Those who believe the Bible is My Word and read it many times do not believe it or apply it to their lives." We understood at a deeper level how David felt when he said in Psalm 119:136, "Rivers of water run down from my eyes, because men do not keep [obey] Your law."

If we have been hurting our Savior friend through unbelief or disobedience, remember, His forgiveness is always extended to a truly repentant heart.

Another way Jesus' faithfulness in friendship was characterized was in rebuking his friends when they were in error.

Because Peter was more outspoken than the others, he was more on the receiving end of this characteristic. There are timeless lessons for each one of us to learn as we look into those occasions. One of Satan's most prevalent and often subtle

7/12/12

tactics is to tempt us to bypass the cross, or death to what gratifies our selfish desires. It simply means to choose the easy way instead of the way God has chosen for us to fulfill our destinies.

When Peter rebuked Jesus by telling Him to bypass His crucifixion, Jesus recognized that Peter was cooperating with Satan's plan to thwart the most powerful event in human history. Jesus responded with the strongest appropriate rebuke in return: "Get behind Me, Satan! You are an offense to Me" (Matthew 16:23). The word *offense* literally means a snare or a stumbling block.

When Jesus was on a high mountain and was transfigured before Peter, James, and John, Peter blurted out the suggestion of making three tabernacles because Moses and Elijah had appeared and were conversing with Jesus. The reaction to the preposterous suggestion of putting Moses and Elijah on the same level of honor as the Son of God caused the Father to rebuke Peter audibly from heaven: "This is My beloved Son. Hear Him!" (Mark 9:7).

Our friend God is still exhorting us today from His Word for spouting out our good ideas of how to serve Him instead of waiting on Him in silence, listening until we hear Him tell us what we're to be doing and when we're to be doing what He says. He tells us clearly in Psalm 62:5 that we're to wait on Him: "My soul, wait silently for God alone, for my

7|12|12

expectation is from Him." And then He promises us clear direction: "I will instruct you and teach you in the way you should go; I will guide you with My eye" (Psalm 32:8).

Jesus rebuked Peter again for trying to get Jesus to avoid the cross. It was when Peter cut off the high priest's servant's ear when they came to arrest Jesus. He responded, "Put your sword into the sheath. Shall I not drink the cup which My Father has given Me?" (John 18:11). Jesus was also preparing Peter for having to embrace the cross (death to self) in his own life, as well as preparing him for how he would eventually die by crucifixion.

How we need to discern from the Holy Spirit, when often the closest people to us don't understand that what God is allowing us to suffer is ultimately for His glory and our good. We need to keep asking our friend the Lord Jesus to rebuke us if we've listened to any suggestions that would tempt us to bypass the cross in any way in our lives.

I am always arrested by the forcefulness of Jesus' rebuke to His friends the disciples over their repeated unbelief. It really got to Him. Accordingly, we should understand how unbelief in our hearts affects our precious Lord. A man whose son was tormented by an evil spirit brought him to Jesus, reporting that he had already taken the child to His disciples but they were powerless to help. We read in Matthew 17:17, "Then Jesus answered and

7/12/12

said, 'O faithless and perverse [unbelieving] gener-
ation, how long shall I be with you? How long shall
I bear [endure] with you? Bring him here to me.'"
Yes, unbelief in the hearts of Jesus' friends made
Him angry.

Now I'm going to give you another illustration
to show you how unbelief makes Him sad. On one
occasion, I was slowly meditating on the Gospel of
John, chapter 1. It happened unexpectedly, when
I came to verse 10: "He was in the world, and the
world was made through Him, and the world did
not know Him." Suddenly the Holy Spirit revealed
to me a portion of the astounding truth I had just
read. The Creator and Sustainer of the entire universe, who spoke and brought into being *everything* and upholds it ALL by the word of His
power, came down to Earth in human form and
was unrecognized and unacknowledged! I broke
into weeping as I experienced a fraction of the pain
of that rejection through mankind's unbelief. But
when I read verse 11, the revelation and the sorrow
increased in intensity: "He came to His own, and
His own did not receive Him." His own nation, the
Jews with their religious leaders, along with His
own brothers, didn't believe Him.

Only those who have experienced the pain of
rejection are able to identify even in the smallest
degree with what it means to feel unvalued. We
can always be assured that our friend Jesus, who

is infinite in understanding, identifies with us at the deepest level. When God has spoken to us in some way about our future, and after a long period of time there is still no fulfillment, let us not insult Him or hurt Him with unbelief. We don't want to add to His pain. A lot more understanding on this subject is given in my book *The Fire of God*.

The next characteristic of Jesus the model in friendship is seen in His pursuing, protective, and caring love for His friends.

When we are tempted to think God has forgotten our address, we need to meditate on the following scriptures:

> "I have told you that I am He. Therefore, if you seek Me, let these go their way," that the saying might be fulfilled which He spoke, "Of those whom You gave Me I have lost none."
> —JOHN 18:8–9

These protective words were spoken when Jesus was about to be led away, prior to His crucifixion. Jesus was fulfilling His promise to His friends then and to His friends now: "I will never leave you nor forsake you" (Hebrews 13:5).

Jesus' concerned love was never more evidenced than when He was speaking about how we should relate to children. Listen to His gentleness in Isaiah

40:11: "He will feed His flock like a shepherd; He will gather the lambs with His arm, and carry them in His bosom, and gently lead those who are with young." Listen to the way Jesus identified Himself and His Father God with them:

> Then He took a little child and set him in the midst of them. And when he had taken him in His arms, He said to them, "Whoever receives one of these little children in My name receives Me; and whoever receives Me, receives not Me but Him who sent Me."
> —MARK 9:36–37

This statement infers that to reject a child is rejecting Jesus. This is emphasized again when Jesus rebuked His disciples for trying to keep people from bringing children to Him: "But when Jesus saw it, He was greatly displeased and said to them, 'Let the little children come to Me, and do not forbid them; for of such is the kingdom of God'" (Mark 10:14). We can often measure our Christlikeness by the value we place on children and how we treat them.

I love to think about Jesus' pursuing love in friendship from the story of the man whom He healed from blindness on the Sabbath day. After the Pharisees had belittled and rejected Jesus and the man, the Bible says that Jesus went and looked

7/12/12

for him until He found him in the temple. Then Jesus revealed Himself more fully to him. What a loving friend.

Perhaps the most poignant picture of Jesus' caring love as a friend would be when He was hanging on the cross in unspeakable agony. He looked down at His devoted mother, Mary, understanding the intensity of her grief-stricken heart. He looked at John, the closest male gift of friendship His Father had given Him. Jesus understood the depth of John's suffering and pain. Jesus knew how desperately these two would need each other in the coming days. And in His infinitely loving, caring, and concerned heart for their needs, He gave them as permanent gifts of friendships to share the same home together. Jesus, our compassionate friend, knows exactly what our friendship needs are for every stage of our lives, and He has a perfect plan to meet them.

Perhaps you're widowed like Mary, or are concerned how you would cope on your own if you became widowed. Whatever it is that concerns us in relation to our being cared for, we can take comfort in the certainty of one thing. Jesus said that He's looking out for and watching over the needs of each little sparrow—and that you and I are of much more value and concern to Him than these little birds. Have you ever seen a worried bird?

7/12/12

If you're still worried about your future, be at rest as you read these wonderful words about the Lord Jesus as a friend: "Having loved His own who were in the world, He loved them *to the end*" (John 13:1, emphasis added). Jesus assures us that He will look after us right to the end of our lives, as we keep worshiping Him, obeying Him, believing Him, and trusting Him.

Another very powerful way Jesus expressed His love for His friends was in the way He interceded for them. In John 17 there are five requests Jesus made to the Father for all of His disciples—past, present, and future.

1. Unity was always His top priority desire for them. It still is for us today. In verses 11 and 21–23, Jesus asks that His disciples be kept through the Father's name and that they may be one as they are one in the Trinity.

2. Jesus asks that His disciples may have His joy fulfilled in themselves.

3. Then He asks that they be kept away from the evil one.

7|\3)/12

4. He goes on to ask that they would be sanctified by the truth of God's Word.

5. Finally, Jesus asks that all His disciples would be with Him in heaven, beholding His glory that the Father has given Him.

For our encouragement, we need to frequently remind ourselves of the amazing promise in Hebrews 7:25: "He [Jesus] always lives to make intercession for them [His disciples]." I sometimes wonder how much expressed gratitude Jesus receives for His faithful, never-ending ministry of intercession on our behalf? I know I, for one, haven't given Him nearly as much as He deserves.

One of the highest expressions of genuine love that I know is to be an intercessor in depth and frequency for the friends God gives us. In my book *Intercession, Thrilling and Fulfilling,* I have devoted chapter 3 to praying for our friends.

Jesus gave understanding to His friends about difficult things.

Only to Jesus' close disciples do we see Him explaining puzzling circumstances and teachings that perplexed them. I love the sentence tucked away in Mark 4:34 that says, "And when they were

7/13/12

alone, He explained all things to His disciples." This was said straight after the sentence that said He only spoke to the crowds in parables. This tells us that those who make the time to pursue the Lord Jesus as an intimate friend can expect Him to reveal His secrets with us: "The secret [friendship] of the LORD is with those who fear Him and He will show them His covenant" (Psalm 25:14).

In Matthew 13:10–23 we find the disciples asking Jesus why He spoke to the other people in parables, and Jesus said, "Because it has been given to you to know the mysteries of the kingdom of heaven, but to them it has not been given" (verse 11). Then Jesus went on to explain to His friends the parable of the sower and the seed.

There is another part of this truth that we must take into consideration. It is a part of God's character that is not taught nearly as much as it should be, but it is one I have already mentioned in this book; that is, the mystery of God (Romans 11:33). This truth also comes out when we look at John 13:7: "Jesus answered and said to him [Peter], 'What I am doing you do not understand *now*, but you will know *after this*'" (emphasis added). Again, we read in John 16:12, "I still have many things to say to you, but you cannot bear them *now*" (emphasis added). Jesus goes on to say in the next verse that the Holy Spirit would come and guide them into truth. So what do we learn from this?

I believe God is saying that it is unwise for us to ask Him what the future holds for each one of us. He alone knows if and when we can handle that knowledge.

It also means that in order to develop us as men and women of faith, God will delay answers to our prayers and the fulfillment of promises He has spoken to us in order to test us to see whether we will trust His character when we cannot trace Him. Job had to do that big-time! Look how God came through in the end—bigger-time!

> My brethren, take the prophets, who spoke in the name of the Lord, as an example of suffering and patience. Indeed we count them blessed who endure. You have heard of the perseverance of Job and seen the end intended by the Lord—that the Lord is very compassionate and merciful.
> —JAMES 5:10–11

These verses also disclose that sometimes God allows some of His closest friends to suffer in order to mentor others in how to go through unexplainably difficult trials triumphantly. He did that not only with Job but also with the apostle Paul. We'll only come through the severity of those kinds of tests if we've taken the time to study God's

7|13|| justice from His Word...as well as all of His other attributes.

All the award-winning medals for servanthood leadership could be heaped upon Jesus the friend— and it still wouldn't do Him justice. Think about the untold hours He patiently taught life-changing truths to the multitudes as well as to the religious leaders, and then continued teaching in greater depth to His disciples. He was always revealing the truth about His Father God and proving in count-less ways that He had sent Jesus, His Son, to Earth to redeem mankind (Luke 24:7).

There's a high price to having a sustained, in-depth, and anointed Bible-teaching ministry. Only those who have paid it will understand what I am saying. In James 3:1 we are given a solemn warning to those who are called by God to teach His Word: "My brethren, let not many of you become teachers, knowing that we shall receive a stricter judgment." The very next verse explains that we are account-able to God in relation to our lives matching up with our words: "For we all stumble in many things. If anyone does not stumble in word, he is a perfect man, able also to bridle the whole body." The word *perfect* here means consummate soundness, whole-ness, maturity, according to Strong's Concordance. Teachers have great influence, and God doesn't want to multiply phonies! We listen to messages that take forty-five to sixty minutes or more to deliver,

7/13/12

and usually have no idea of the many hours or days of preparation and prayer God required before that message could be given with authority.

Jesus' servanthood also showed up in extraordinarily practical ways. The more we ponder His majestic splendor, blazing glory, awesome holiness, and limitless power, the more we marvel that He showed up at dawn one morning on the beach with a hot breakfast all prepared for His close friends. I am impressed. The preparation would go something like this. He would have bought the bread ahead of time, caught the fish from the shore, gathered the firewood and coals together, made sure there were plates, utensils, cooking oil, and a frying pan...oh, and the salt and the matches—minimum. (See John 21:9, 13.) I am not even coming to consciousness at that hour of the morning let alone operating in a full-blown ministry of hospitality—outdoors! What a friend and chef! If we think that's impressive, then how about this scenario?

We have to keep in mind that the actions about to be described come from the ruling, reigning monarch of the universe. Otherwise we miss the point.

We must also understand the circumstances surrounding this incredible display of humility. The emotional traumas are overwhelming when we really think deeply about what Jesus was experiencing and facing.

7/16/12

Jesus was in full knowledge that His close friend Judas was about to betray Him. The Master was facing Peter's denial of Him and being forsaken by all His disciples. He was facing the agonies of Gethsemane plus the scourging, scoffing, humiliation, and brutality of men's satanic inspired hatred in full force.

In that setting, the King of glory in human flesh took a basin, poured water in it, and washed and dried each of the twelve disciples' feet. Then Jesus gave these clear instructions to them and to us: "If I then, your Lord and Teacher, have washed your feet, you also ought to wash one another's feet. For I have given you an example, that you should do as I have done to you" (John 13:14–15). Verse 17 emphasizes this command with this powerful addition: "If you know these things, blessed are you if you do them."

Could anything be clearer? Hardly! So why in the world is this injunction so seldom obeyed? Could it be that humility of heart is what God sees as our greatest need and has set up a vital way to meet it? Think about it. Some of the most historic and significant moves of God's Spirit that I have been in (and there have been many) have been in times where this command has been obeyed.

During a ten-day GO Festival in Durban, South Africa, Youth With A Mission International combined forces with many denominations in

7/16/12

Durban. We had an international team of speakers who spoke to the thousands who attended. The theme was world evangelization. We had powerful times of praise and worship and intercession for the nations, as well as evangelistic outreaches in the streets.

A significant highlight of those glorious days was when we had a massive foot-washing service. Unity among all believers had been emphasized in the teaching time. Now it was being demonstrated. Blacks, whites, Africans, Zulus, Indians, and numbers of people from different denominations were all one in Christ Jesus—many said for the first time—in this unique setting.

Everyone was instructed to ask the Holy Spirit to direct them to another person of a different race. Then they were to sit at that person's feet and wash them, speaking the love of the Lord to them. After that they were to wait on God, seeking Him for directions as to how to pray for the person's deepest needs to be met and to then pray it out in faith. Because God is so practical, He showed us that the foot washing could easily be carried out by using baby wipe cloths. It was so simple and effective.

It is impossible to adequately describe the spiritual dynamics that took place on that historic occasion. God's manifest presence was palpable, with signs and wonders being demonstrated amidst the

7/16/12

flow of tears of emotional and physical healings and racial reconciliations. Some of heaven came down to the earth that day.

This next aspect of Jesus as an encouraging friend is closely connected with His servant-hood.

Although Jesus had to often rebuke Peter, Jesus delighted in encouraging him. After Peter had declared, "You are the Christ, the Son of the living God," Jesus gave Peter full marks by saying, "Blessed are you, Simon Bar-Jonah, for flesh and blood has not revealed this to you, but My Father who is in heaven" (Matthew 16:16–17).

When a woman lavished her devotion on the Lord Jesus by pouring expensive fragrant oil on His head, He gave her the most encouraging response of all time! "Assuredly, I say to you, wherever this gospel is preached in the whole world, what this woman has done will also be told as a memorial to her" (Matthew 26:13).

We can only fully appreciate the magnitude of that encouragement and affirmation when we realize that Jesus said in Matthew 24:14, "And this gospel of the kingdom will be preached *in all the world* as a witness to all the nations, and then the end will come" (emphasis added). That means that this woman's unabashed, extravagant, unself-conscious outpouring of intense love to the Lord

7/16/12

Jesus will be known by every people group on Planet Earth. Wow!

Then I love the fact that Jesus made a point of publicly honoring a poor widow who gave everything that she had into the offering box. She would hear His words of approval, and it would be all the encouragement she needed to believe that somehow He would see that her needs would be met. When I get to heaven, I want to look her up and hear her story. I often think about it, and it intrigues me. She gave—so, of course, it would be given unto her.

A Gentile army officer really got Jesus' attention one day, to the point that the Bible says Jesus marveled at this man's strength of faith. The centurion told Jesus that he had a servant in desperate need of healing, and Jesus said He would go to the man. But the centurion replied that would be entirely unnecessary, as he believed all Jesus needed to do was to speak the word, and the healing would be accomplished. That's when Jesus was impressed and said publicly, "Assuredly, I say to you, I have not found such great faith, not even in Israel!" (Matthew 8:10). How encouraged that humble, faith-filled military officer would have been to hear those words.

Perhaps there's a strong leader to whom God wants you to give an encouraging word today. Ask Him to show you. There's no telling what it could mean to that one. Perhaps there's an act of kindness that would bring enormous encouragement

7/16/12

to someone through you. I will never forget when Jesus brought huge encouragement to my husband, Jim, and myself through one of His and our dear friends. His name is Leland Paris, a leader in Youth With A Mission.

For many years I had been asking God to bring us out of debt from the mortgage on our home. We have lived entirely by faith since 1971 when we joined YWAM, knowing that no salaries are given. I hadn't the faintest idea how God would answer those persistent prayers of faith. But I plugged away. Jim also carried this burden in prayer.

We were attending a YWAM International Staff Conference in the Philippines, where I was a speaker. At age sixty-five, Jim had recently survived complicated major heart surgery and had been clearly directed by God to relinquish his position on YWAM's International Leadership Council. He had just as clearly been led by the Holy Spirit to merge his ministry giftings with mine. I desperately needed his help.

We were on the conference platform, where YWAM leaders were graciously honoring us, when it happened. We both experienced the delighted shock of our lives when dear Leland Paris presented us with a check for $25,000. We were immediately debt free. What an unforgettable moment! What a faithful God! What an encouraging friend!

7/16/12

Leland had, completely unbeknown to us, managed to collect names and addresses of friends of ours from around the world. He had written, asking them to consider contributing to a fund to bless us financially. Some were in YWAM; others were from a list of people who prayed for us regularly. We will forever be indebted to a precious servant-hearted man who responded to a prompting of the Holy Spirit and, by so doing, went to a lot of effort to encourage us, his fellow missionaries. Our gratitude is also very deep for all those who contributed to that fund, enabling us to experience the unbelievable freedom of being out of debt. What precious, encouraging friends.

Now we look at Jesus the friend who enters into our sorrows and understands our suffering.

The first reason is because Psalm 147:5 says God is infinite or unsearchable in His understanding. That means that because of His infinite knowledge of everything related to our circumstances, there is no limit to the depth of His ability to understand what we're going through. That's a major source of comfort and cause for us to stop and thank Him—right now.

The second reason that He understands our suffering is because He suffered more than anyone else: "He is despised and rejected by men, a man of sorrows and acquainted with grief. And we hid, as

it were, our faces from Him; He was despised, and
we did not esteem Him" (Isaiah 53:3).

What an enormous comfort to know that whatever grief we may have to go through, or however
horrendous the circumstances we may find ourselves
in, our precious Lord has already been through it. So
He goes beyond having compassion for us—He identifies with us in our pain. That brings us to understand how He functions as our High Priest before
God on our behalf:

> For it was fitting for Him, for whom are
> all things and by whom are all things, in
> bringing many sons to glory, to make the
> captain of their salvation perfect through
> sufferings.
> —HEBREWS 2:10

> For we do not have a High Priest who cannot
> sympathize with our weaknesses, but was in
> all points tempted as we are, yet without sin.
> —HEBREWS 4:15

Finally, I want you to understand how sensitive Jesus is as a friend.

He never forced Himself on His disciples. When
Jesus was walking along the road to Emmaus with
two of them, after His resurrection, we read in Luke
24:28, "Then they drew near to the village where

7/16/12

they were going, and He indicated that He would have gone farther." It was only when they invited Jesus to come into the house that He accepted and ate food with them.

At the same time, the amazing truth is that Jesus wants our friendship and is lonely without it. He created us for intimate friendship with Himself. In John 6:67 we hear Jesus saying to His close disciples, after many had turned away from following Him, "Do you also want to go away?" Jesus cared so much about whether Peter really loved Him, He asked Peter that question three times!

Song of Solomon 7:10 tells us eloquently about Jesus' love for us: "I am my beloved's, and his desire is toward me." And again in Song of Solomon 6:3, "I am my beloved's, and my beloved is mine."

He's the friend who gives us the biggest challenge and the biggest reward. He says:

> If anyone desires to come after Me, let him deny himself, and take up his cross daily and follow Me. For whoever desires to save his life will lose it, but whoever loses his life for My sake will save it.
>
> —LUKE 9:23–24

The reward is intimate friendship with the most exciting, mysterious Being in the universe. He works me hard, tests me severely, but spoils me rotten. He's the only One who can totally fulfill me. He's King God, the lover of my soul.

APPLICATION OF THIS TEACHING

1. Are you honestly modeling your life on the Lord Jesus Christ as outlined in this teaching?

2. Have you really studied His life from the Bible?

3. As a way of life, do you stop and ask the question "What would Jesus do?" when you're not sure what is the right decision to make?

4. Do you recognize your need to have God-given friendships as Jesus modeled?

5. Does your lifestyle reveal that you're committed to having the same characteristics in friendships with others as Jesus had? All? Some?

6. Are you pursuing a more intimate relationship with Jesus to ensure that you'll be a more Christlike friend to others?

7/19/12

7. What are the characteristics of Jesus'
   life as a friend that need to be applied
   more to your life?

   - Forthrightness in communication,
     not ambiguity or vagueness

   - Godliness and naturalness with
     both sexes

   - Unconditional love

   - Servanthood

   - Thoughtfulness to meet practical
     needs or do menial tasks for
     others

   - Total forgiveness to those who
     have wronged us

   - Faithful to communicate future
     events, one who doesn't habitually
     bring last-minute information

   - A tireless teacher of truth

   - Friendships with the lost to bring
     them to Christ

7/19/12

- An encourager to the strong and not so strong

- A faithful intercessor

- Protective, caring, and concerned love that is communicated to our friends when they are suffering

- Faithfulness to bring correction in humility, gentleness, and love where needed

8. Ask God for conviction and revelation where you're failing to live as Jesus modeled the leader friend for us, and repent in brokenness before Him.

9. Determine, with the Holy Spirit's enabling, to become more conformed to the image of Jesus.

Chapter Six

JESUS THE MASTER SOULWINNER

Because Jesus is our role model in everything, we need to study His earthly life closely to understand why He was so successful in bringing others into His kingdom. Jesus, as the Son of man, operated on the following basic principles.

The first principle was to fulfill the purpose of doing the Father's will: "For I have come down from Heaven, not to do My own will, but the will of Him who sent Me" (John 6:38). In Luke 19:10 we read what that was: "For the Son of Man has come to seek and to save that which was lost."

The apostle Paul had in-depth revelation of the implications of those words; that's why he could

7/19/12
8/30/12

respond by saying, "And He died for all, that those who live should live no longer for themselves, but for Him who died for them and rose again" (2 Corinthians 5:15). In Jesus' typically simple, forthright style He gives all His disciples an uncomplicated mandate: "Follow Me, and I will make you fishers of men" (Matthew 4:19).

Sheer logic demands that we conclude that witnessing to people and, at times, winning them to the Lord Jesus is an automatic outcome of following Jesus. What else could it mean? Conclusion: if we're not sharing our faith with those who don't know Jesus, we're not fully following Him.

A major purpose in finding and following Jesus is to get others to find Him and follow Him. So, let's get real and answer the obvious question before the Lord. Are we fulfilling that purpose as a way of life? Listen to the apostle Paul's burning challenge:

> Awake to righteousness, and do not sin; for some do not have the knowledge of God. I speak this to your shame.
> —1 CORINTHIANS 15:34

I remember being impacted by the testimony of an elderly man who was a famous Bible teacher and author. Nearing the end of his life he was asked what he would do differently if he could live his life over again. His immediate reply was, "I would share

7/19/12
8/30/12

my faith in Christ with the lost far more often than I did." Sobering thought. Wrong priorities.

We shouldn't have to be driven to witness to others out of a sense of guilt or because we know it's something we should be doing. It should be a natural part of daily living. It was so with both my parents as I was growing up.

My dear mother would witness to nearly everyone who came to the door of our house. As the stores were a long way from where we lived, and she had no car, the tradesmen would regularly call for their orders, and then on another day deliver them. This was normal for most people in New Zealand at that time.

During the course of giving the tradesman the grocery or meat orders, Mother would make a cup of tea for the man, give him a gospel tract my dad had written, testify to the reality of Christ in her life, and pray for the person's needs. She was also always reaching out to the poor and needy in every practical way that she could. She lived the gospel that she shared.

My dad was a wonderful evangelist, Bible teacher, and pastor who, like Paul, worked for his living. Unlike Paul, my dad had a wife and five children to support. But, like Paul again, he witnessed about the reality of Christ and preached the gospel at every given opportunity—in churches, over the radio, in written form, in personal evangelism. To

8/30/12

me, as a child, evangelism was never an event; it was a normal way of life. It was as normal as eating and sleeping!

What a heritage. What a privilege. What accountability. "For everyone to whom much is given, from him much will be required; and to whom much has been committed, of him they will ask the more" (Luke 12:48).

The outcome of this normalcy was to witness to my close friend at school and lead her to Christ when I was ten years old. Later as an adult and a parent, she testified to the reality of her conversion at that particular time in her young life.

As the Master Soulwinner, or the bearer of the truth about Himself as the Way, the Truth, and the Life, the second principle Jesus operated on was to live in submission and obedience to the Father's orders. It was the only way He could fulfill His goal.

Jesus never attempted to win the lost without the Father's specific directions:

> Most assuredly, I say to you, the Son can do nothing of Himself, but what He sees the Father do; for whatever He does, the Son also does in like manner. For the Father loves the Son, and shows Him all things that He Himself does.
>
> —JOHN 5:19–20

The immediate application to our lives comes again from Jesus' words, "As the Father has sent Me, I also send you" (John 20:21). In order to live lives of submission, dependence, and obedience to Jesus, we need to have unhurried time daily alone with God in His Word, the Bible. We need to be listening to His voice, obeying what He says. We need to be worshiping and praising Him.

It is also essential that we be empowered by the Holy Spirit to be effective in evangelism. We can rely on the wonderful promise in Acts 1:8: "You shall receive power when the Holy Spirit has come upon you; and you shall be witnesses to Me."

On a daily basis we need to ask God to convict us of any sin and repent of anything He reveals to us. Then we thank God for His forgiveness. Matthew 5:6 says, "Blessed are those who hunger and thirst for righteousness, for they shall be filled." Ephesians 5:18 gives us a command to be filled with the Spirit. We come to God, realizing our great need to be empowered for His service. When we have fulfilled the above conditions, we come to Him and ask for His Spirit to come upon us and control us completely. Then we receive in simple faith that He will. And He does.

The supernatural gift of a word of knowledge (1 Corinthians 12:8) is often a very powerful means God uses to bring a non-Christian to becoming a declared follower of Christ. This gift, along with

other gifts, is an outcome of having been empowered by the Holy Spirit; the gifts are given by God
sovereignly as He wills, according to 1 Corinthians
12:11. The following remarkable testimony from Bob
Maddux, senior pastor of Christian Life Assembly,
Poway, California, illustrates this point:

> In the fall of 1964, after graduating from
> high school the previous spring, I headed off
> to college in the San Francisco Bay area. I
> soon found myself deeply immersed in the
> budding counterculture that was emerging
> in that region. It wasn't long before I was
> experimenting with drugs and the "hippie"
> lifestyle. This soon led to an increasing in-
> quisitiveness about spiritual alternatives.
> "Trips" on LSD and other hallucinogenic
> drugs caused me to encounter spiritual
> dimensions that I had never experienced
> before. I had attended various churches as I
> was growing up, but for the most part I had
> remained unmoved by the typical "churchi-
> anity" I came across.
>
> One day in late December of 1966 I had an
> experience on LSD that shook my idealistic
> world. The supernatural suddenly became
> a very scary place. I stumbled upon what
> appeared to be the evil side of this drug-
> induced domain. You could say that I had

a face-to-face with the demonic. One thing for sure was that I came to believe that the supernatural realm was real. But when I held up my "experience" in this dimension against what I'd found in church, the church came up sorely lacking.

Christians had been witnessing to me, but it all seemed like just words—kind and interesting words, but still just words. By the fall of 1967, after an odyssey that had led me from Big Sur to the desert town of Joshua Tree, California, I found myself back in my hometown of Chico in a state of apathy. I felt that after all my "searching," I'd come up empty. It was then that I was invited to a meeting in a home near the college campus. I was told that there was a nineteen-year-old preacher speaking that night. That in itself appeared as a complete anomaly to me. Most of the preachers I'd seen or heard had been older men who were for the most part completely irrelevant to me. I was fascinated and attended the meeting with a more than usual level of curiosity. That night my life was about to change forever.

When I sat down with the other twenty-five college kids that night, I was first struck by the wonderful singing that filled the small apartment. There was an unusual fervency in

8/30/12

the way they expressed their hearts to God in song. I had never heard anything like it.

Then I began to sense real nervous stress, almost as if every nerve was on fire. Some force seemed to want me out of that room. The sense of discomfort was intense, and it took all of my willpower to remain seated. But I was determined not to let on to the others around me what I was going through. In the past I had practiced various forms of meditation. So I tried to practice peaceful contemplation, appearing to all around me to be in a state of "bliss." I was confident that my real state was going unnoticed.

It was then that the young nineteen-year-old preacher stood up and began to address the students. I'd never seen him before. His name was Mario Murillo. He had short-cropped hair, dark eyes, and wisdom beyond his years. The first thing I remember him saying once he was on his feet was this: "There's someone in this room right now, and you're very nervous in your body." As simple as that phrase sounds, there was something truly profound in it. It was as if unexpectedly this young man had looked inside my soul. It was as if God had lifted the roof off the building and pointed His finger at me and said, "I'm real." There was no way that Mario could have known that this was exactly what I was going through at that moment. But suddenly I knew that God was there...that there was a God of power and knowledge that knew all about me, right down to the internal struggles that I was hiding from the world around me.

I raised my hand and acknowledged Mario's words. He asked me to sit in a chair in the middle of the room. I was trembling all over my body and was under deep conviction of sin. Mario told me that God was showing him that there were three evil spirits that I needed to be delivered from and that as I surrendered to God, deliverance would come. I was desperate and cooperated. Mario cast out those demons in the name of the Lord Jesus, marveling at how quickly I was set free. This was his first experience in this kind of ministry.

Mario told me to repeat a prayer asking Christ into my heart as my Lord. The prayer included words of repentance as I renounced the other religions and philosophies with which I had been involved. I acknowledged that Jesus was the Truth. I was making a clear distinction between Christ, the true Light, and the false light I had followed before. Mario then prayed for me to be baptized in

8/30/12

the Holy Spirit. The power of God touched me, and I was soon praying to God in another language. This seemed to just explode from deep within me, and although it was only a few words at first, within a few weeks it became a clear, distinct, and fluid expression of the Holy Spirit's gift.

The supernatural power of God, through the word of knowledge, had broken the spell of deception over my life and brought me almost instantly to an understanding that the God of my youth was a God of power who could outmatch any supernatural power of the evil one. Now thirty-nine years later, after nearly thirty-six years in full-time ministry, I'm hungrier than ever for the reality of God's power to flow through my life to touch a world looking for a "God who is there."

We also need to be praying that God will lead us to the lost He wants us to reach. I have found that when I am stirred up in my spirit, longing to win the lost to Christ and looking for those opportunities, that's when the exciting witnessing adventures come my way! When I get passive about witnessing, those opportunities just don't seem to show up. Or perhaps it's because of spiritual dullness that I'm not able to recognize them. This is all too easy to occur!

The following story is meant to encourage the reader that God has prepared hearts everywhere, in the easily accessible places, who are longing and waiting for us to open our mouths and gossip the gospel with them...if we will ask Him to lead us to them. It's so natural. So needed. So easy under the Holy Spirit's direction and control. And so utterly thrilling and fulfilling.

My husband, Jim, and I were having dinner on a Saturday evening at an Iranian restaurant near our home in California when we started asking the new young waiter questions about himself. He quickly disclosed that he was a twenty-year-old Iranian, spoke the Farsi language, was studying aeronautical engineering at college, and working part time at the restaurant to pay for his education. We noticed he was unusually focused about serious issues and that he welcomed our genuine interest in him as a person. In fact, the warmth of our approach seemed to cause him to open up to us in a remarkably short time.

In fluent English he shared that although he was Iranian, he wasn't a Muslim, having recently become a Coptic Christian attending an Armenian church. Students at his college had witnessed to him about Christianity. We immediately told him we were followers of Jesus Christ, had lived as missionaries since 1970, and as such had traveled the world extensively, and were thrilled to know he was a new believer in Christ.

But it was the next piece of information that totally stunned him. We told him that we knew an evangelical Farsi-speaking pastor and congregation who met together every Sunday, who were all Iranians, and who were vital and alive in the power of the Holy Spirit. We had to keep repeating it over and over again before he could finally accept it as truth.

We then said we would take him with us to this church service the very next day, which we did. The service started at 1:00 p.m. It is one of a number of ethnic church services that are part of The Church On The Way, in Van Nuys, California. After the service, Babbak (named Bob in the United States) shared with us that his seventeen-year-old sister, Anahita, had come to Christ when she was twelve years old in Germany, prior to their family coming to the United States. A Christian neighbor had taken Anahita regularly to a Baptist Sunday school. He also said that neither his father nor mother was a Christian.

Bob's mother, Mary, was so grateful that someone had befriended her son, she told him to bring us into their tiny apartment after the service, as she wanted to meet us and give us hospitality. We found a precious, very lonely, middle-aged woman who could speak Farsi and German but hardly any

English, while Bob and Anahita were amazingly fluent in English, considering the short time they had lived in the States.

We stayed for many hours listening to her story (interpreted for us by her two children) as she showed us many family photos. We then shared the way of salvation with her and left her with it clearly outlined in a brochure I have written titled "A Committal of Life to the Lord Jesus Christ." We told her how welcome and loved she would be at the Farsi-speaking church.

During the afternoon I put my arms around her and told her I loved her. She immediately burst into tears and had to leave the room until she could regain her composure. She was craving love and acceptance in this foreign land and often suffered depression. Her response to our love was to call us mother and father. It was with great reluctance that she finally received a monetary gift (they were in great financial need), and we had to convince her that it went with the family relationship God had just given us with them.

That week Jim and I prayed much for Mary's conversion. The following Sunday she went to the Iranian church service with Bob, and at the end immediately responded to the invitation to receive Jesus as her Lord and Savior. She attended a number of classes where she learned the scriptural implications of baptism by immersion, and she was subsequently baptized. She enthusiastically joined the women's Bible study classes and hasn't missed the Sunday service in years. The change in Mary's countenance and life was, and is, deep and real—a total transformation.

We were very aware that the bigger and harder-to-catch fish for Christ in this precious family was Carmi, the husband and father. We couldn't get him to attend the Farsi church because his job as a valet car parker at a restaurant demanded that he work seven days a week.

We would go regularly to the little apartment and have vital fellowship with Mary, Bob, and Anahita. Mary would prepare wonderful Iranian food while her two children would ask us questions by the hour about the Bible and the Christian faith. Discipling them was thrilling. They were so eager to learn.

Very beautiful, highly intelligent Anahita would fire questions at me at an unusually rapid rate, such as:

"Have you had anything to do with demons?"

"Yes."

"Have you ever cast them out of anyone?"

"Yes."

"Tell me about it."

I would relay an incident.

"Tell me another case."

I would do so.

"Have you heard God speak to you?"

"Yes."

"How many times?"

"Too many to remember or count."

"How did He speak to you?"

"In numbers of ways."

"Tell me one of them."

I would share an incident.

"Tell me another one."

This type of conversation would continue *nonstop*. I have never seen such a hunger to learn spiritual truths.

Other times they would come to our home. On one occasion we were able to introduce them to an outstanding Youth With A Mission missionary who had suffered greatly during solitary confinement in a top-security Iranian prison for nine weeks because of his faith in Christ. He still has a great love for the Iranian people. Bob is highly intelligent, intense, very polite, and passionate about his generation and culture finding purpose for life in Christ. Who knows whether God has a purpose in the future for linking these two together in missionary work?

After many weeks of fervent prayer for Carmi's conversion, we found ourselves again in our friends' little apartment late one Saturday night, waiting for Carmi to come home from his valet parking job. We had met him once before when the family came to our home. We found him to be a very like-able person who had expressed great gratitude for the many ways we had helped them materially. He knew we genuinely loved him. Friendship evangelism with practical assistance had laid the groundwork for what was to follow.

It was about midnight when Carmi came home. In front of his family and Jim, in a relaxed, loving way, I shared the claims of Christ with him—that Jesus is the Son of God. I explained that He took the punishment for our sins upon Himself by His death on the cross and His resurrection. If we repent of our sins, ask for His forgiveness, and invite Him to come and live within us, He will do both and give us eternal life according to God's Word, the Bible. I also made clear the importance of surrendering our wills to Him and acknowledging His lordship openly to others. Then I asked Carmi what he was going to do with the Lord Jesus. I will never forget his decisive answer: "Give my life to Him! Why not?" In front of us all, Carmi carefully prayed aloud every word of the comprehensive prayer on the brochure I had given him, committing his life to Christ.

We explained the necessity of getting a job that would enable him to go to church with his family, yet understanding how difficult it was for him to find work—along with the language struggles. But this new convert meant business with God. For many months, the only church service he could possibly attend was at 8:00 a.m. on Sundays at the English-speaking service at The Church On The Way, because he had to be at work by 11:00 a.m.

As Carmi put God first, God made a way for him to obtain a much better job where he had every Sunday off, enabling him to attend the Farsi church with his family. His pastor told us how impressed he is with Carmi's strong faith and ardent worship. He never misses a service and absorbs the teaching of God's Word. He has since attended many weeks of instruction related to the scriptural implications of water baptism and the need to be empowered by the Holy Spirit and has been water and Spirit baptized.

Another thrilling time at our Iranian family's little apartment was when we were all together with their daughter Anahita's new husband, whom she met at the Iranian church, together with his family, along with Mary's brother from Chicago. There were eleven of us. What a night to remember!

Mary's Iranian brother kept asking us highly intelligent, strong questions about the meaning of life and eternal issues. As both Jim and I depended entirely on the Holy Spirit for answers, His wisdom flowed between us without a hitch. It was exhilarating.

While we were all partaking of Mary's sumptuous meal, I turned to Anahita's new father-in-law, who was seated next to me, and simply asked the question, "Have you ever had a personal encounter with the Lord Jesus Christ?"

"Yes," he replied. "He came to me in a dream. I saw Him standing in front of a door, and He was knocking on it. He looked at me but never said anything. Then I woke. I have never forgotten it but never understood it."

"Oh," I said. "That's very significant. I can help you to understand the purpose of that encounter." Turning to Revelation 3:20 in my Bible, I asked him to read aloud Jesus' words of invitation to open the door of our hearts to Him so that He can come and enter, take up residence, and have fellowship with us, eternally. This man of sixty-two years had never heard this truth and was eager to learn more. I grasped the opportunity by presenting to him the way of salvation. I took him through the Scriptures and steps as outlined on my "Committal of Life to Christ" brochure.

I told him that at midnight, about six months previously, in this same room, Carmi had responded to Christ's invitation and had experienced a totally changed life. Carmi then testified to that truth and went on to share how on two recent occasions he had woken up with severe pain in his thigh and legs and could hardly walk. He immediately called on the Lord to help him, and both times he had received a miraculous healing. The older man's response to all this was to pray to the Lord, in front of everyone in that room watching and listening, his prayer of commitment to Christ, and to acknowledge Him openly as Lord and Savior.

While this was taking place, Jim and I noticed how his thirty-year-old daughter was listening intently. She asked, "Is it possible to hear God's voice? Does He communicate with people?" Jim cashed in on her sincere search for truth and went and sat beside her and had a marvelous time presenting the claims of Christ to her. He gave her a copy of my book *Forever Ruined for the Ordinary: The Adventure of Hearing and Obeying God's Voice*, which has the way of salvation clearly outlined at the back. Jim was convinced of her sincerity and remarked on the very intelligent, well-thought-out questions she kept asking him. Her brother, Arish, has since said that she read the book and commented very favorably on its contents.

We got to bed at 2:30 a.m. that Sunday morning, so elated it was hard to sleep. I'm convinced that there are countless numbers of lonely foreigners, struggling to learn the language, struggling financially, whom God sends to our shores in the United States. His plan is to expose them to the life and liberty in the Lord Jesus Christ. He longs for us, His children, to have a burden for their lost souls, to have compassion for their hardships and heartaches, and to reach out and be His arms extended to them through friendship evangelism.

I can't think of anything more thrilling or rewarding than when we cooperate with God's plan. We do ourselves the greatest favor and are blessed beyond words. It's not complicated. Just ask God on a daily basis to bring the people across the pathway of your life to whom He wants you to witness and to help become disciples. And then obey the promptings of the Holy Spirit when He does. I can guarantee you'll be ruined for the ordinary. At the same time, heaven will be more populated and hell less.

The following things characterized every encounter Jesus had with a lost soul:

- He had a deep concern for their immediate condition as well as for their eternal welfare. His compassion was manifest by meeting them at their deepest point of personal need. His was never a computer-style approach.

- Jesus was compelled to witness to each one the Father directed Him to, regardless of the personal cost to His reputation or His comfort.

- Praying to His Father during the course of meeting human needs was a way of life (Luke 5:15–16).

- He was empowered by the Holy Spirit (Luke 3:21–22).

- Jesus had a burdened heart for the lost. This was the strongest motivation to reach them. And it will be the same with us, if we're going to be effective.

We can accumulate a lot of statistics about how many people are unevangelized. We can study methods of evangelism. We can be part of the most highly developed programs related to personal and mass evangelism. We can be witnessing out of a sense of obligation to God and spiritual leaders who tell us we need to be doing so. We can preach messages on the need to reach the unreached...*and never have any or little burden for the lost,* resulting in being relatively ineffective in reaching people for Christ; whereas a person with a God-given burden for the lost will inevitably be effective, without necessarily having any involvement with all the above things just stated.

STRATEGIES FROM JESUS' LIFE AS A SOULWINNER

Jesus' first strategy is that He went out to where the people were, which means that most of His soul-winning was done outside the synagogues. He didn't expect the people to come to Him in the temple. He went to them.

He found the Samaritan woman by a well at lunchtime. He found fishermen Andrew, Peter, James, and John down by a lake. He found tax collector Matthew during his course of doing business. He found wealthy tax collector Zacchaeus up a tree in the streets of Jericho and talked to him later in his house. He found the blind beggar Bartimaeus on the roadside. He found the demon-possessed man from the Gergesenes down by a lake. He found the man blind from birth, in John 9, while walking along the road.

What is the significance of all this to us? The answer is found in Luke 9:1–2:

> Then He called His twelve disciples together and gave them power and authority over all demons, and to cure diseases. He sent them to preach the kingdom of God and to heal the sick.

The next verses make it very clear that *they were to go out to where the people were.*

> And He said to them, "Take nothing for the journey...." So they departed and went through the towns, preaching the gospel and healing everywhere.
>
> —LUKE 9:3, 6

These verses also make it equally clear that praying for the sick was an automatic part of presenting the gospel. We can never improve on Jesus' methods of evangelism, simply because that's the way He modeled it.

I was deeply moved when I read the following recent account of how this works in Jim Green's report in relation to how a young evangelist in Campus Crusade for Christ presented the gospel in a Muslim village with the *JESUS* film.

> Our team was doing about six outreaches a week in the bus (in a very tough location). We were headed for a large village and sent a co-worker ahead to arrange a meeting with the chief, to ask his permission and announce the showing of *JESUS*.
>
> When I arrived, the worker was trying fruitlessly to persuade the chief. He wanted nothing to do with *JESUS* and declared,

"I am a Muslim, I am a Muslim leader. I lead the mosque, and I'm the chief of the village. Since this village has existed, we have never allowed any other religion. You will do *nothing* here!"

With the Holy Spirit as my guide, I respectfully replied, "We are coming here to show you and your people the *JESUS* film, preach the gospel, and heal the sick."

He responded, "What did you say? Heal the sick? Really? Is that possible?"

"Yes, if you allow us to show the *JESUS* film and preach the gospel."

He looked at his second-in-command and fell silent. There was a pause as he thought. The chief turned back to me and said, "Really? Heal the sick? OK, we want to see this." With his permission, the film team went to work at a large soccer field. They unloaded the projection equipment and generator, threaded the film, and set up the screen, speaker, and lights. Then they went about announcing the film.

Around five thousand people came that night and filled the soccer field. *It was standing room only.* Something was happening. As the projector started, I went to the car and prayed, asking God to give me a word for these people when the film concluded.

They were deeply moved by the *JESUS* film. So much was literally foreign to them, yet so wondrous. They were stunned by the life of the good Man, His crucifixion and resurrection. [He is describing the power of the Word of God on which the film is totally based, a message that penetrated deep into their souls.]

The people were listening in a way I've never seen in all the outreaches. I felt like the Holy Spirit was hovering over the entire soccer field and village, calling them out of darkness. His presence was so strong.

Over the microphone I called out, "How many here recognize a need for a Savior?" Almost everybody raised his hand. There was a group of young people on my right. Some raised their hands and voice, "We want our sins to be forgiven!" Then others on the side cried out, "We want our sins to be forgiven!"

Everyone began crying out to God for mercy. So, in that moment, I led the entire group of five thousand in the prayer of salvation. Then I spoke to the crowd. "This Jesus is not only a Savior, but He is a Healer, and today He wants to heal anybody who is sick. Bring your sick forward." So, one by one, they came—first about twelve men and women with back problems. He healed them all, instantly. They brought a young deaf boy, about eight years old. The Lord healed him. People kept coming and kept being healed. God was at work affirming His Word and His Son! It was simply incredible.

On my right stood the chief, the leader of the village and the mosque. Now I turned to him and said, "Do you see what is happening?"

He answered, "Yes. Can I say something to my people?" I gave him the microphone and he stepped forward. To the five thousand he spoke, "What you have just seen is real because there is no man who can do what you have seen unless God is with him and with these people who have come to us. The Lord is with them. Now, bring all the sick from the village! *Go home now and bring them here!*"

As I continued to pray for the people, a father came running. He was holding his daughter. She was seven years old, born totally blind. He pleaded with me, "Please pray for my daughter."

I said, "Do you believe Jesus will heal her?"

He answered, "That's why I brought her!" I prayed and then moved my hand across her face. She started to move and followed my hand. She was able to see.

She moved her head to the left, to the stage and lights. She was just amazed by the lights and everything she was seeing. She was still in her father's arms, and he asked her, "Do you see? Do you see?"

She turned her eyes to him, and looked on her father's face for the first time in her life. She knew his voice but had never seen his face. The look on both their faces was amazing. She answered, "I can see you."

Our God is so wonderful! That day the people saw the gospel lived out before them through these affirming miracles and through the *JESUS* film in their own language. They experienced the living Word of God that reached into their hearts, the Word that the Holy Spirit used to open their hearts to know God.

Because I believe this part of Jesus' life and ministry in reaching the lost is so important, I am going to give you another example—from the ministry of Campus Crusade for Christ, with the use of the *JESUS* film, taken directly from the Gospel of Luke. Again, the setting was in a resistant, mostly Muslim area.

The people became enraptured with the story, the miracles of Jesus, His atoning death and glorious resurrection. They were gripped by the concept of His love and forgiveness, ideas that were very foreign to them.

When the DVD ended, an evangelist stood on a truck and spoke to the crowd. He preached the gospel again and proclaimed a verse the Lord had given him, Mark 9:23 (NIV): "Everything is possible for him who believes."

A crippled man in the back of the crowd cries out, *"I believe that I can walk again!"* Heads turned...and all eyes were on the man. The crowd fell silent. Slowly, the man began crawling with his arms to the front. Tears rolled down his cheeks as he kept crying out, *"I believe...I believe...I believe!"*

When he at last made his way to where the evangelist stood, the evangelist looked at him with great compassion and commanded, *"Walk, in Jesus' name!"* Then God intervened. As an astonished crowd looked on, the man stood, took one step, then another, and another. He was walking for all to see! The Word of God was confirmed. They realized that Jesus was the true and living God. That night many indicated decisions for

Christ and were delivered from deception and darkness.

A leader of this team tells us that moments like this are common, since the teams have regularly used only a DVD and a projector. She reports there is often "mass response and rich excitement... *that people press in on us after the showings, wanting prayer. Crowds shout their approval as the blind and dumb receive their sight and hear again, affirming that this Jesus, whom they have heard speak their own language, is truly God. After the meetings hundreds of new believers entreat us to 'please build a church here. We don't want to follow our former religion anymore.' In this area God has used JESUS to plant churches in village after village!"*

There are now 988 different translations of the *JESUS* film.

The second strategy that Jesus used to win the lost is that He was always sensitive to the Father's promptings as to the wisest approach for each individual. And it varied greatly. For example, when blind Bartimaeus, the beggar, was crying out for mercy on the roadside, Jesus met his physical need for eyesight first. Then we read that he immediately followed Jesus, glorifying God. How wonderfully that same method of meeting human need has been used worldwide for effective evangelism. Samaritan's Purse Ministries, the numerous mercy ministries operating throughout YWAM worldwide, and the numerous orphanages and AIDS ministries internationally, to name just a few, prove this point.

It is fascinating to see the totally different strategy Jesus took with the rich young ruler. (See Luke 18:18.) In his case Jesus told him that following Jesus would take selling all he owned and giving the proceeds to the poor. This was only because Jesus saw that this man's greatest need was a revelation of the love he had for his wealth and possessions, in relation to eternal issues and values.

Then we see another strategy Jesus had with the demon-possessed man from the region of the Gadarenes. (See Mark 5:1.) Jesus sensed the man's great desire to be delivered, so He first cast out the legion of demons. Then the man expressed a great desire to stay with Jesus as His follower. But Jesus told him to go home to his friends instead and tell them what great things the Lord had done for him and how Jesus had compassion on him.

This story really shows how we must not presume upon methods but seek God for His specific strategy for each individual, because usually it is wiser to make sure that the person's will is committed to making Jesus Lord before freeing them from demonic spirits. How utterly fascinating Jesus is.

Finally, let's take a look at Jesus' strategy with Nicodemus, a member of the Jewish council and a leading teacher of the Old Testament. Jesus' approach couldn't have been more direct; it went straight to the heart of the man's deepest need. Jesus said, "Most assuredly, I say to you, unless one is born again, he cannot see the kingdom of God" (John 3:3).

Jesus didn't philosophize with this learned rabbi or enter into theological discussions with him. He gave him the simplest possible gospel message: "For God so loved the world that He gave His only begotten Son, that whoever believes in Him should not perish but have everlasting life" (John 3:16). Take it or leave it.

So what do we learn from Jesus' strategies? Only the Holy Spirit knows what is the jugular vein of need in each person, and He will simply direct us to the approach that matches that need as we depend entirely upon Him to direct us moment by moment during our encounters with needy souls. It's called walking on the water. It's exhilarating. And only God can get the glory, because it's totally supernatural. Hallelujah!

I love the next story that comes out of the missionary organization I belong to, called YWAM. A student who was in training at one of our Discipleship Training Schools, which happened to be in Holland, was out in the streets of Amsterdam one day when she came across a young man sitting on the pavement in obvious great need...in every way. Prompted by the Holy Spirit to approach him, with a burdened heart for his lost soul, she gently and simply said, "You need the Lord Jesus."

She then proceeded to buy him a hamburger and took him to a store and bought him some new clothes. Finally she invited him to go with her the next day to an evangelistic meeting where, for the first time, he heard the way of salvation. He was blown away by this demonstration of the life of the Lord Jesus in this young woman, accompanied by being confronted with how his life could be transformed by giving it to the One who he learned was the Way, the Truth, and the Life. John Goodfellow chose to become a true follower of that One, the Lord Jesus Christ.

Several years after John had been through YWAM training schools, he became one of YWAM's most effective outdoor evangelists, with demonstrations of God's miracle-working power being displayed in the salvation of souls and the healing of bodies. I know. I have stood in the streets and have heard and seen it happen. In fact, he was the leading evangelist in that ten-day outreach in the streets of Durban during the GO Festival in South Africa that I wrote about in an earlier part of this book.

The third strategy of Jesus' life as a soulwinner is that He is our greatest example in cross-cultural and interracial interactions. The classic example would be His dialogue with the Samaritan woman at the well. Both the disciples and the woman were amazed to discover Him, a male Jew, talking to a female Samaritan. Neither of these things was *ever* done culturally.

It is interesting to note that Jesus broke through that cultural and racial barrier by asking her to do Him a favor by giving Him a drink. In His humility He declared His need of her help! As a Jew, who never had anything to do with Samaritans, Jesus was breaking all traditional and cultural rules. But Jesus isn't affected by men's prejudices. He was compelled to witness to this woman regardless of the inevitable misjudgings of men—and regardless of the personal physical cost. Jesus was tired, thirsty, and hungry after a long walk. And it was lunchtime.

Father God revealed to His Son, Jesus, how His request to her for water was the perfect lead into the subject of her spiritual need for the water of life. Through the conversion of an influential, immoral woman, a whole city is reached with the gospel, and many are converted. Surely she was a most unlikely potential evangelist.

Neville and Wendy McDonald are the senior pastors of Healing Word International Church in

Los Angeles, California. They are dear friends of mine, and we have spent many hours sharing the wonders of how God works, period! They are seasoned in pioneering churches in cities. I was fascinated to learn from them that whenever they are sent by God to a new location, they ask God to lead them to the most influential person in the town and the most notorious. The purpose is to win them to the Lord first. It sounds like Jesus had the same strategy.

However, we must never rationalize who are the most influential people to reach a city for Christ but obey the promptings of the Holy Spirit in witnessing. It was straight after winning this woman to Himself as a disciple that Jesus said, "Lift up your eyes and look at the fields, for they are already white for harvest!" (John 4:35).

The most unlikely people in our human reasoning can be used by God to bring the biggest harvest of lost souls into His kingdom. Think about the man from the region of the Gadarenes from whom Jesus cast out a legion of demons. As a direct result of his going back to his region, called the Decapolis (which means ten cities), and witnessing to the power of his deliverance, the Bible says that all the people were amazed. This man's remarkable testimony had a profound effect upon ten cities. In the accounts that are written in Matthew 4:25 and Mark 7:31, we find that there was a great stirring in that region in relation to Jesus' ministry, and many followed Him.

God wants to get the following truth through to us from both of these ordinary people who had personal encounters with our extraordinary Jesus: He has prepared hearts *out there*, right now, today, in our everyday circumstances, waiting for us to give them the resurrection message He gave to Mary Magdalene, "Go and tell them I'm alive and have revealed Myself to you." They're waiting to hear. They're wanting answers. They're desperate. Their hearts will be responsive. They're in hotels and apartment buildings, in homes, in the streets, on the beaches, in offices, in the stores and supermarkets, at gas stations, on airplanes, in bars, in restaurants.

Listen to the heart cry of God from Joel 3:13–14:

> "Put in the sickle, for the harvest is ripe.
> Come, go down; for the winepress is full,
> the vats overflow—for their wickedness is
> great."...For the day of the LORD is near in
> the valley of decision.

It is important for us to understand that our model, the Lord Jesus, was never impressed or intimidated by the varying levels of society a person came from. He was always God-the-Father conscious, therefore never self-conscious.

While Jesus was having a meal in the home of a religious leader, an ex-prostitute gate-crashed the dinner party and poured out her lavish devotion on Jesus in gratitude for the forgiveness He gave her of her many sins (Luke 7:36–50). Jesus was obviously totally unembarrassed. He was equally relaxed with each of these differing levels of society and that they were together with Him.

Jesus didn't hesitate to rebuke the religious host for his incorrect judging of Jesus by letting her continue her display of affection to Him. And then He pointed out the coldness of the Pharisee's self-righteous heart toward Him.

Jesus always went right to the point where the person needed the greatest revelation of his or her need to repent of sin. The Holy Spirit will give to us that knowledge as we seek Him and expect Him to release it to us. It is a very important key in personal evangelism and can save hours of time.

The final strategy I want to share with you from Jesus' life as a soulwinner is that He never led anyone to believe that it was a light decision they were making to follow Him—because it wasn't the truth. He knew that unless they counted the cost and totally committed their lives to Him, they could never be His disciples. Jesus made the cost very clear. Listen to His words in Luke 14:27: "And whoever does not bear his cross and come after Me cannot be My disciple." Verse 33 reiterates this truth by stating, "Whoever of you does not forsake all that he has cannot be My disciple."

That simply means we need to give up the right to do our own thing. It means that all that we have is His, and He has the right to tell us what we're to do with anything at anytime. It means the big sellout to Him. We abandon the right to make our own decisions. It's a total takeover by Him, at our request.

If you think that's scary, my response is this: think about whom you're abandoning yourself to— all knowledge, infinite wisdom, absolute justice, unswerving faithfulness, awesome holiness, limitless power, and unfathomable love. That represents the ultimate security. I do myself a favor by running to Him and saying, "Hey, take over...fast!" It's scary NOT to!

In realism, we also find that Jesus tests us all along the way. It's all part of becoming a true disciple. The more intimate we become in friendship with Him, the greater the tests. This is very evident from studying God's Word. Look at the incredible tests from God that Job, Abraham, Moses, Joseph, David, Mary (the mother of Jesus), Hannah, Esther, Daniel, Paul, and the apostle John endured. Books could be written on their rewards, because God is absolutely righteous and just.

We have already observed that Jesus was the friend of sinners. Listen to the lineup.

- The Samaritan woman at the well who had five husbands and was living in adultery

- The woman whom the religious leaders brought to Him who was caught in the act of adultery

- The ex-prostitute in Simon's house

- Zacchaeus, the crooked tax collector

Have we friendships with unconverted people for whom we are praying on a regular basis? Are we living a Christlike life in front of them? Are we witnessing to them about the reality of Christ in our lives? Statistics prove that the majority of people are converted and discipled one on one in friendship evangelism.

APPLICATION OF THIS TEACHING

Where we know we are not like Jesus as the master soulwinner, we need to confess and repent of the *causes*, which will be revealed as we answer the following questions.

1. Have you real spiritual ambition for the extension of God's kingdom and therefore a real burden for the lost?

2. Are eternal issues the deepest concerns of your life?

3. Are you preoccupied with your own ambitions, needs, and problems and therefore not involved with the lost?

4. Are you preoccupied with the responsibilities of your other ministries to the exclusion of witnessing and personal soul-winning?

5. Have you ever faced the fact that just as we're usually born to reproduce natural children, we're born again to reproduce spiritual children through the on-coming power of the Holy Spirit as we witness to and pray for the lost? What are you doing with that responsibility and accountability?

6. How often do you have an effective witness to non-Christians?

7. Are you pursuing non-Christians in friendship to win them to Christ?

8. How many lost souls have you led to the Lord personally? Many? Few? None?

9. When was the last time you led a soul to Christ?

10. Have you a list of lost souls for whom you regularly pray? If so, does it increase regularly in numbers?

11. Jesus said the gospel must first be preached to all nations, and then the end will come (Mark 13:10). Because Mark chapter 13 is related to the second coming of the Lord, does your present way of life hasten or hinder His coming?

12. Are you sincerely concerned about the answers to these questions?

SUGGESTED PRAYERS OF REPENTANCE
WHERE APPLICABLE

Almighty God, I acknowledge my lack of a true burden for the lost—my prayerlessness and lack of involvement with them. I humble myself before You and acknowledge my great pride that manifests itself in living contrary to the priorities and principles by which Your Son in His great humility lived by when on Earth. I acknowledge the idolatry in my life that has manifested itself in being more concerned in doing my own thing than Your thing. I repent of the sin of disobedience to these truths in Your Word. I choose to become desperate to become a witness and a soulwinner.

A suggested frequent prayer

Lost sinners are dying in darkness today,
And no one seems willing to show them the
    way.
O fill me with passion and vision I pray;
Make me a winner of souls.

Make me a winner of souls,
Make me a winner of souls,
Lead me, I pray, to someone today.
Make me a winner of souls.[1]

In my book *Intercession, Thrilling and Fulfilling*, you will find much more inspirational teaching and illustrations, with guidelines as to how to pray effectively for many other vital subjects.

Chapter Seven

JESUS THE MODEL AS THE LION

Satan's main ministry, whether to the body of Christ or to the unconverted, is to try and give a distorted view of God—His character and His personality.

This teaching from God's Word will help to thwart the possibility of that distortion. It grieves me when I think of the many churches throughout the world that portray the Lord Jesus in sculptures and pictures hanging limp and lifeless upon a cross—the emblem of weakness. Whereas the reality is that our precious Savior and sin-bearer, having paid the full penalty for the price of our redemption, cried out on the cross the triumphant words, "It is finished."

After His death and bodily resurrection, having commissioned His present and future disciples to go and evangelize and disciple all nations in the power of the Holy Spirit, He ascended into heaven and is seated at the right hand of the Father, interceding for His own. Therefore we need to think of Him as the all-conquering King God, the ruling, reigning monarch of the universe.

In order for us to understand some of the wonders of this amazing and utterly unique person of the Godhead, let us look into these two opposite aspects of His personhood. In this chapter, we'll start with His likeness to a lion. Revelation 5:5 describes the Lord Jesus as "the Lion of the tribe of Judah," being the only one who could "open the scroll and to loose its seven seals." This depicts supreme authority.

The prophet Malachi strongly predicted that the Lord Jesus would come and expose the sins of unrighteous offerings that would be made among God's people and the ensuing judgment that would follow (Malachi 3). This prophecy was dramatically fulfilled when we read about Jesus early in His public ministry.

He went into the temple, and operating with boldness and fearless lionlike takeover, He drove out the money changers with a whip of cords and overthrew the tables. "He said to those who sold doves, 'Take these things away! Do not make My Father's house a house of merchandise!'" (John 2:16). Jesus told them that His Father's house was meant to be a house of prayer for all nations, but they had made it a den of robbers (Mark 11:17).

This incident portrays the roar of the lion among the other beasts, letting them know that it doesn't pay to mess with him when they are on his territory. This aspect of strength is described in Proverbs 30:30: "A lion, which is mighty among beasts and does not turn away from any." Jesus was portraying the righteous wrath of His Father as men were desecrating the place where God's glory was meant to be manifest.

The Bible has some significant things to say about God roaring as a lion:

> A lion has roared! Who will not fear? The Lord
> GOD has spoken! Who can but prophesy?
> —AMOS 3:8

Again, we read in Hosea 11:10:

> They shall walk after the LORD. He will roar
> like a lion. When He roars, then His sons
> shall come trembling from the west.

There are rare occasions, such as we have seen in Jesus' public ministry in the temple, when the Holy Spirit manifests God's strong displeasure to a given situation among His people through a God-appointed, anointed, spiritual leader. That leader operates in the fear of the Lord, devoid of the fear of men, with a loving heart, full of spiritual ambition for the people to whom he is exhorting, and with a burning desire for their good and for the extension of God's kingdom.

The outcome is always positive, when every one of those conditions is fulfilled. We read:

> He who boldly reproves makes peace. The mouth of the righteous is a fountain of life.
> —PROVERBS 10:10–11, RSV

On one memorable occasion I had the great privilege of seeing this truth demonstrated. It was when we were living in Auckland, New Zealand, and were members of the Hillsborough Baptist Church. The pastor was the Reverend Hayes Lloyd. He was a former president of the New Zealand Baptist Union. At the time of this incident, he had only been the pastor of this church for three months.

As a way of life, I would intercede fervently throughout the week that my pastor would have a clear understanding what the word of the Lord was that was to be given to the people from God's Word, not just some good message of truth. In the process of this committed intercession, during one week, I received clear impressions that God was going to require Hayes Lloyd to speak out with boldness some very difficult things. I had zero knowledge what they were. I shared this only with my husband, Jim, and fervently and frequently prayed for the fear of God to be upon our pastor, enabling him to be released from the fear of men.

At the following Sunday morning church service, Hayes Lloyd spoke a good message from Romans 16, where Paul honored a long list of his fellow workers who labored with him in the ministry. About ten minutes before the close of the message, I whispered to Jim, "This is *not* what I have been burdened in my spirit about all week!" So I pressed into God with more silent, intense prayer as Hannah did in the temple. I couldn't bear for us all to miss God's strategic purposes (whatever they were).

Then it happened! Abruptly and without any warning, our beloved pastor said, "That's the end of the message. But it's not the end of the service." Immediately I nudged Jim and said, "Here it comes, darling" (with immense relief and an indescribable sense of excitement and anticipation).

For the next awesome ten minutes, with boldness and authority like Elijah on Mt. Carmel, that precious servant of God roared like a lion as he called the whole church to "rip up the labels" that were causing division among us...the labels called Baptists, Charismatics, Pentecostals, Evangelicals, etc. He called us to be "all one in Christ Jesus" with intensity and fervency. To manifest true repentance and brokenness before God and man, he asked us to kneel on the floor in humility and do business with God. You could have heard a feather drop on a velvet cushion! The impact was palpable!

The silence was only broken by the weeping of the people repenting of their sins, some on their knees and some lying on the floor. God had come in response to a man of God who paid the price to be like His Master, confirming the words of Proverbs 28:1: "The wicked flee when no one pursues, but the righteous are bold as a lion." Hayes Lloyd had had a personal renewal in the Spirit, allowing God to do a deep work of bringing change in his own life first, before calling the people he shepherded to do the same.

That morning made significant history in the life of that church, from which we were later commissioned and sent out into world evangelization. And Hayes and May Lloyd became two of our dearest and closest friends.

Back to Jesus. As I have studied this subject from God's Word, I have found fourteen occasions in Jesus' life where He brought strong rebuke to others. It was either to the Pharisees or to His disciples. There is nothing easy about confrontation. I dislike it immensely. But I know that God will hold us accountable in a coming day if we have not paid the price to help others in their spiritual development. If they are not living up to the biblical standards and they are under our sphere of leadership, we should gently and lovingly coach them, along with much encouragement, to see it and make the changes.

Jesus didn't leave His disciples in any doubt about how He felt when they wanted to call down fire from heaven in judgment on the Samaritans who had rejected Jesus' ministry:

> And when His disciples James and John saw this, they said, "Lord, do You want us to command fire to come down from heaven and consume them, just as Elijah did?" But He turned and rebuked them, and said, "You do not know what manner of spirit you are of. For the Son of Man did not come to destroy men's lives but to save them." And they went to another village.
>
> —LUKE 9:54–56

A person with a humble, compassionate heart will always ask God for mercy to be extended to those who reject Jesus, even though God may have pronounced judgment on them. This was the secret of Moses, the greatest intercessor in the Old Testament. I love the verse in James 2:13, "For judgment is without mercy to the one who has shown no mercy. Mercy triumphs over judgment."

Jesus taught, "Blessed are the merciful for they shall obtain mercy" (Matthew 5:7). I have observed over my long lifetime that those who are judgmental and merciless to others are, at some later time, inevitably found in difficult circumstances themselves...crying out to God and wondering why their prayers are not being answered. Pride is always the basis of a merciless heart. Were it not for God's mercies, we would all be consumed. (See Lamentations 3:22.) God owes none of us anything...at any time. Period.

In Luke 11:52 Jesus makes a very strong statement to the lawyers in His time. We hear Him publicly rebuking them in His lionlike boldness as He says, "You have taken away the key of knowledge. You did not enter in yourselves, and those who were entering in you hindered."

Nothing of what I have written should ever give anyone license to vent his or her personal anger or frustration on an audience. That will be met with God's displeasure and only distance a shepherd from his flock. In the instance I have cited in this section, the man of God was moving in the fear of the Lord, devoid of the fear of men, and his life and ministry were characterized by love.

We need to have deep understanding and clear insight as to why Jesus manifested Himself so strongly as the Lion of the tribe of Judah to the teachers of the Law (the scribes) and the Pharisees. He couldn't tolerate them, to put it mildly. They were the one section of society that He spoke to with vehemence. No kidding. Listen to His words.

After Jesus had delivered a demon-possessed man from a spirit of blindness and muteness, the Pharisees accused Jesus of being demon possessed. His response was, "Brood of vipers! How can you, being evil, speak good things?" (Matthew 12:34).

In Luke 11:37–54 we read about Jesus rebuking the Pharisees for having outward rules about hygiene but having no concern for the purity of their hearts. In verses 39 and 40 He describes them as "foolish ones, whose inward part is full of greed and wickedness." Jesus then goes on to rebuke the Pharisees, the scribes, and the lawyers for their pride, hypocrisy, lack of justice, and lack of love. He finishes by making this pronouncement. "You have taken away the key of knowledge. You did not enter in yourselves, and those who were entering in you hindered."

Again, in Mark 12:38–40 and Luke 20:45–47, we read about Jesus rebuking the scribes for pride, hypocrisy, legalism, lack of justice, lack of mercy, and lack of fidelity. In Matthew 23:27–36 Jesus calls the teachers of the law and the Pharisees whitewashed sepulchers, serpents, and offspring of vipers, and then He pronounced heavy future judgment on them. Wow! How much more displeasure could Jesus disclose?

In Matthew 16:3 Jesus rebuked the Pharisees and Sadducees for their spiritual dullness in not being able to discern the signs of the times—their inability to interpret spiritual truths.

In order for us to understand the measure of raw courage and outrageous boldness that Jesus had in addressing these religious leaders in His day in the way He did, we need to understand how they were viewed by the people. The scribes and the Pharisees were an elite group of society who were believed to be the ultimate authorities related to interpreting the Law, Israel's sacred literature. Nobody questioned their status, and they were extremely influential. They were very legalistic and were locked into their traditions. Mark 7:3 called it "the tradition of the elders," and woe to anyone who so much as questioned any particle of those traditions.

The One who is Truth saw behind the masks of phoneyism, inconsistency, and sheer hypocrisy and cryptically announced, in essence, "Don't do what they do, because they don't practice what they preach." (See Matthew 23:3.) Jesus then declared that not only were they the "least" in the kingdom, but they were not even in at all. In Matthew 5:20

Jesus said, "For I say to you, that unless your righteousness exceeds the righteousness of the scribes and Pharisees, you will by no means enter the kingdom of heaven." The result of this kind of exposure motivated this group of society to incite the people to call out, "Crucify Him!…Crucify Him!" (Mark 15:13–14).

How does all this apply to us? The easiest thing in the world is to be blind to the "Pharisee" that can so easily be in any one of us. That's why I think we need to frequently check the list of things that characterize a pharisaical spirit.

First, let's stop and ask the Holy Spirit to reveal to us where we may be guilty, and need to repent, as we go over the following list. He will answer every honest, sincere prayer.

- Teaching truth but living differently from that truth (Matthew 23:3)

- Trying to make others believe we are something that we are not (Matthew 23:14)

- Elevating ourselves in our own minds above others (Luke 18:13–14)

- Having an outward form of right behavior but having unrighteous thoughts (Matthew 5:21, 28)

- Being motivated by the love of money rather than by God's priorities (Luke 16:14)

- Being legalistic by keeping the traditions of men while overlooking matters of compassion and mercy (John 9)

- Making sure other people know when we do charitable deeds, fast, and give monetarily to others (Matthew 6:1–4, 16–18)

- Pointing out other people's faults but being blind to our own (Matthew 7:1–5)

- Being jealous about those who are in more prominent positions than we are or who have greater advantages than we have (James 3:14–16)

- Making the traditions of men a priority rather than living by the

principles in the Word of God
(Matthew 15:16–20)

- Judging by outward appearances
  (Matthew 23:5) instead of leaving
  the judgment to God, who judges by
  the heart motivation (1 Samuel 16:7)

- Being more concerned with what
  men think about our actions than
  what God thinks. The Pharisees
  sought the praise of men more than
  the praise of God (John 5:44). It
  revealed their fear of men and their
  lack of the fear of God.

- Making a big deal out of things of
  minor importance while overlooking
  things of major importance. Jesus
  called it "straining at a gnat, but
  swallowing a camel" (Matthew
  23:23–24). It meant neglecting
  things like caring for the poor and
  showing kindness to strangers and
  the disenfranchised in society.

- Making excuses for neglecting to
  honor and take care of parents by
  giving the provisions and monetary

gifts they deserved to other religious or Christian causes (Matthew 15:5–6)

- All *unrighteous* judging of others— period. Matthew 7:1 says that whenever we judge another, we automatically will be judged by God. That's heavy duty. We do ourselves the greatest favor by keeping our big mouths shut tight when making conclusions on other people's actions.

Only God has 100 percent knowledge of every person's situation. Only God knows the up-to-date record of every human heart. Even if people were proven to be guilty, how do we know whether or not they may have totally repented a few minutes before we pronounced our judgment? Titus 3:2 says, "To speak evil of *no one*, to be peaceable, gentle, showing all humility to all men" (emphasis added). Humility makes the difference, as I will illustrate.

I was profoundly moved when a friend of mine shared with me the revelation he had on the mercy of God toward him. I realized I needed a far greater revelation of that aspect of God's character and immediately sought God for it.

Many years ago, as a spiritual leader, my friend indulged in gross sins and went far away from God.

He left the ministry and lived in open rebellion to Him. As a result of God's great *mercy* and the prevailing, persistent prayers of godly, loving intercessors "who would not let God go" on his behalf, he finally deeply repented of his sins and returned with his whole heart to the Lord. For three whole months he wept before God daily in repentance and true brokenness of spirit and gratitude as God showed him everything that he needed to acknowledge and turn away from. During this time God also revealed to him the hurts from his past for which he needed to receive God's healing love and comfort that were not related to his sins.

He then told me that anything God gave him in addition to the salvation of his soul, he considered as an extra coming from God's mercy— whether it was a cup of cold water, a bed, a friend, or clothing—anything!

This revelation of God's mercy leaves no room for murmuring, only a constant spirit of gratitude coming from deep humility of heart.

King Nebuchadnezzar obviously had a great revelation of the mercy of God coming from the depth of his repentance over persisting in the sin of pride. He was then able to give one of the finest testimonies of God's absolute justice in relation to the severity of punishment he had received from God, which was his reason being taken from him and having to eat like an animal.

I don't believe we have to commit the sins these two leaders did in order to have their revelation of the mercy of God.

Mercy is not getting what we deserve. Grace is getting what we don't deserve.

Too many times we look for evidences of God's justice toward us instead of acknowledging that it's "through the LORD's mercies we are not consumed" (Lamentations 3:22).

Obedience is living in the light of revealed truth. All else is disobedience. "Therefore, to him who knows to do right and does not do it, to him it is sin" (James 4:17). If God were to let us see a list of our sins of omission, let alone our sins of commission, as He sees them, we would not only have a greater understanding of His mercy but we would also be marveling at the extent of His grace toward us.

Deeper revelation of these truths will be released to our minds by prayerfully and carefully reading through Psalm 78. In true humility we will identify with the children of Israel. Remember, one sin of presumption is rebellion against God! We did "our own thing" without seeking His face for direction.

In 2 Corinthians 7:9, Paul says, "Now I rejoice, not that you were made sorry, but that your sorrow led to repentance. For you were made sorry in a godly manner."

Our repentance level of sin is so shallow because we do not have a "godly grief" over our sin; therefore, we so often think God owes us more justice than mercy. Humility makes the difference in our perspective.

Up to now we have been dealing with unrighteous judgment. The Bible teaches there is also a time for righteous judgment: "Do not judge according to appearance, but judge with righteous judgment" (John 7:24).

Prophecy is to be judged, according to 1 Thessalonians 5:19–21:

> Do not quench the Spirit. Do not despise prophecies. Test all things; hold fast what is good.

First Corinthians 14:29 clearly reiterates the same truth: "Let two or three prophets speak, and let the others judge."

Another time for righteous judgment is when we are in positions of spiritual leadership and have to deal with people where it is proven that they have erred. When that is so, we must follow the clear biblical guidelines related to handling those situations.

An audiocassette tape of my teaching on "Immorality From God's Viewpoint" is available from my Resource Guide, referenced at the back of this book. This message also covers the biblical principles involved with how leaders are to deal with any kind of sin in those who have erred.

I have given another message that is a powerful deterrent in keeping people from falling into sin, titled, "Phoneyism, Inconsistency, and Hypocrisy." It is available from the same source.

Chapter Eight

JESUS THE MODEL
AS THE LAMB

B ecause John the Baptist's description of the
Lord Jesus was, "the Lamb of God who takes
away the sin of the world!" (John 1:29), this title
must be very important to the Godhead. In 1 Peter
1:18–21 we read:

> ...that you were not redeemed with cor-
> ruptible things, like silver or gold...but with
> the precious blood of Christ, as of a lamb
> without blemish and without spot. He [Jesus]
> indeed was foreordained before the founda-
> tion of the world, but was manifest in these
> last times for you who through Him believe

in God, who raised Him from the dead and gave Him glory, so that your faith and hope are in God.

This means that before Creation, the Godhead agreed on a plan that if man chose to sin and come under God's judgment, then Jesus would become the substitute and shed His blood, making atonement for our sins, for those who would appropriate that atonement.

In the Book of Revelation alone, there are twenty-eight references to the Lord Jesus Christ as the Lamb, all of which greatly exalt Him.

Think about the cacophony of sensational sound and the kaleidoscope of spectacular color that would emanate from the historic scene that is described in Revelation 5:11–14:

> Then I looked, and I heard the voice of many angels around the throne, the living creatures, and the elders; and the number of them was ten thousand times ten thousand, and thousands of thousands, saying with a loud voice:
>
> "Worthy is the Lamb who was slain to receive power and riches and wisdom, and strength and honor and glory and blessing!"
>
> And every creature which is in heaven and on the earth and under the earth and such

as are in the sea, and all that are in them, I heard saying:

"Blessing and honor and glory and power be to Him who sits on the throne, and to the Lamb, forever and ever!"

Then the four living creatures said, "Amen!" And the twenty-four elders fell down and worshiped Him who lives forever and ever.

Cecil B. DeMille wouldn't even come close in attempting to portray that mind-boggling scene. That right has been reserved for the Lamb of God. He is the only one worthy of this kind of magnificent splendor and transcendent glory being attributed to Him.

In God's governmental dealings with mankind, the way down is the way up. And no one who was so far up chose to go so far down as Jesus, the Son of man. So that meant that He had to be given the highest place of honor by the highest authority, Father God.

A lamb is young, tender, and dependent on others. It isn't characterized by being aggressive or clever—just submissive. This portrays the total submissiveness Jesus operated in at all times to His Father's directions, portraying the ultimate in humility.

But Jesus' humility is portrayed in an even deeper way through His vulnerability in becoming a human. Think about the implications of Deity in diapers! The One who spoke and the universe was created subjecting Himself as a helpless baby, dependent on the creatures He created to feed Him and sustain Him. Majesty personified meekness as He exposed Himself to the weakness and vicissitudes of the mortals He created.

We can only grasp a fraction of understanding of this incomprehensible humility by thinking of what it would be like for us to become ants and to subject ourselves to the ramifications of the ant world. Unthinkable! Yes, it's entirely beyond all rationale. But that's because we know so little of what humbling ourselves is all about. And it's what God is the ultimate specialist in doing and being.

Meekness is harnessed strength. We see this lamblike nature being manifest in Jesus as a twelve-year-old boy. The first glimpse of Him is found in Luke 2:40: "And the Child grew and became strong in spirit, filled with wisdom; and the grace of God was upon Him." The next description is in verses 46–47: "After three days they found Him in the temple, sitting in the midst of the teachers, both listening to them and asking them questions. And all who heard Him were astonished at His understanding and answers."

Remember, we're talking about the One who is

infinite in knowledge and wisdom as we continue to read in verses 51–52: "Then He went down with them and came to Nazareth, and was subject [obedient] to them....And Jesus increased in wisdom and stature, and in favor with God and men."

Again we see the evidence of this harnessed strength as Jesus submitted Himself in baptism to the ministry of John the Baptist. Immediately after that, He submitted to the suffering of being tempted by the devil in the wilderness. One of the most amazing scriptures to me is found in Hebrews 5:8: "Though He was a Son, yet He learned obedience by the things which He suffered." We will never comprehend or appreciate the extent of Jesus' humility and meekness until we understand the marvels of His majestic splendor and glory.

If I chose to become an ant, to reach ants, and to give them eternal life, I would at least expect to be recognized for who I was before stooping to those lengths of condescension. Not Jesus! And then I would probably remind them from time to time who I was as I subjected myself to their lack of knowledge and wisdom and their frailties. Not Jesus. My spirit bursts into song as I try to recall the refrain of the hymn we used to sing at my home church in New Zealand:

O what a Savior is mine.
In Him God's mercies combine

His love can never decline
And He loves me![1]

Now let's look at Jesus the model as the Lamb
in the various ways He handled unjust accusations. His methods were not stereotyped, so ours
must not be either. There was a time many years
ago when I thought it was wrong to ever try and
explain my innocence when unjustly accused,
believing that in time God would vindicate me
based on Isaiah 54:17: "No weapon that is fash-
ioned against you shall prosper, and you shall
confute every tongue that rises against you in
judgment. This is the heritage of the servants of
the LORD and their vindication from me, says the
LORD" (RSV). The motivation was right, but I was
ignorant of Jesus' ways related to this subject and
therefore imbalanced in this area.

First we'll see Jesus answering His accusers with
a simple direct explanation. In Matthew 9:11–13,
Jesus was accused of keeping bad company: "Why
does your Teacher eat with tax collectors and
sinners?" He answered with a statement of purpose
related to His mission on Earth: "I did not come
to call the righteous, but sinners, to repentance."
In Mark 3:22–30, after Jesus was accused of being
possessed by Beelzebub, the prince of demons, He
explained how this could never work. He warned

them of the great seriousness of attributing the work of the Holy Spirit to the work of the devil.

On the next three occasions we find Jesus ignoring the accusations made against Him and continuing on in ministry.

1. In John 7:20, after Jesus was accused of being possessed of a demon, He ignored the comment and went on to explain the rightness of healing a man on the Sabbath day.

2. In John 9:16 we find that after Jesus had healed a blind man on the Sabbath day, the Pharisees said, "This man is not from God for He does not keep the Sabbath." Jesus ignored their accusations and then sought out the man and revealed Himself to him as the Son of man.

3. In Mark 3:21 Jesus was accused of insanity by His friends. He ignored the comment and went on answering another accusation.

So there are times when the Holy Spirit will direct us to overlook the inevitable times when we will be wrongly judged. I always take great comfort in God's promise in Psalm 103:6: "The LORD executes righteousness and justice for all who are oppressed." God does it in His way and time if we will forgive the offender by receiving God's grace.

Next we see Jesus confronting His accusers (the Pharisees) with a full-blown explanation of Himself following their blatant accusations. It is found in John 8. In verse 39, the Jews said, "Abraham is our father." Jesus responded, "You are of your father the devil, and the desires of your father you want to do. He was a murderer from the beginning, and does not stand in the truth, because there is no truth in him. When he speaks a lie, he speaks from his own resources, for he is a liar and the father of it. But because I tell the truth, you do not believe Me. Which of you convicts Me of sin? And if I tell the truth, why do you not believe Me? He who is of God hears God's words; therefore you do not hear, because you are not of God" (verses 44–47).

But after the Jews charged Jesus with having a demon, He calmly denied it and went right on teaching them and explaining His origin and source of authority: "Before Abraham was, I AM" (verse 58). They tried to stone Jesus, but He escaped.

There were times when the apostle Paul also boldly stated the truth about his citizenship, life, and ministry before his accusers. Acts 22 and 23 has that account. It is significant how God responded His approval in Acts 23:11: "But the following night the Lord stood by him and said, 'Be of good cheer, Paul; for as you have testified for Me in Jerusalem, so you must also bear witness at Rome.'"

Next we see Jesus as the silent Lamb before His accusers. He was always reacting in obedience to how the Father directed Him—hence nothing stereotyped. The Holy Spirit will always be faithful to prompt us when to be silent and when to speak when we are unjustly accused. In John 18 and 19, we find that after declaring that He was the King of the Jews, Jesus was scourged, then accused of treason. Jesus was silent. He gave no answer. The result: crucifixion.

There may well be times when we are obedient to the Holy Spirit by being silent before our accusers that we will suffer also. But we serve a magnificent Master who is "righteous in all His ways, gracious in all His works" (Psalm 145:17). He is the Ultimate Accountant who is keeping the records and will surely vindicate us, as long as we do not hold resentment in our hearts to our accusers.

If we will not receive by faith God's miracle-working love in our hearts to forgive our accusers, we will not be forgiven the many things by God for which we need His forgiveness. If Jesus and Stephen could ask Father God not to lay the sin of their murderers to their charge, can't we receive by faith that same miraculous love and grace to forgive our accusers?

Jesus continued to be silent in the face of being accused of blasphemy after stating simply that He was the Christ, the Son of God. After the high priest pronounced death as the judgment, Jesus was spat upon in His face and beaten. His reaction was silence (Matthew 26:62–68).

This is a time to pause and pray one of the prayers of the hymn writer Thomas O. Chisholm, who wrote "O to Be Like Thee."

> O to be like Thee! Lowly in Spirit,
> Holy and harmless, patient and brave;
> Meekly enduring cruel reproaches,
> Willing to suffer, others to save.[2]

In John 18:33–37, when Pilate questioned Jesus about His kingship, Jesus clearly stated, "For this cause I was born, and for this cause I have come into the world, that I should bear witness to the truth. Everyone who is of the truth hears My voice" (verse 37). Later, in John 19:9 when Pilate asked Jesus, "Where are You from?" Jesus gave Him no answer.

Jesus' authority was always deafening, whether it was in spoken words or in silence, because He was operating under obedience to the Father's orders. That's why Jesus wasn't threatened by Pilate's question, "Don't You know I have power to release You and power to crucify You?" Pilate thought he was in control. Jesus knew God the Father was in control, horrendous as the circumstances were.

Similarly, when we are totally surrendered to the Lord Jesus at all times, He takes full responsibility for us, no matter how difficult the circumstances. What relief! That's when "Be still, and know that I am God" (Psalm 46:10) is particularly meaningful.

We continue to see Jesus being silent under questioning before the governor when the chief priest and elders accused Him of many things. It is best summed up by quoting from *The Life of Christ in Stereo*, which combines Luke 23:2–3, Matthew 27:11–14, and Mark 15:2–5:

> But they began to accuse Him, saying, "We found this fellow perverting the nation and forbidding to give tribute to Caesar, saying that He Himself is MESSIAH, a King." And the chief priests and the elders continued to accuse Him of many things. But He answered nothing. Then said Pilate to Him, "Do You answer nothing? Do you not hear how many things they are charging against you?" But Jesus still answered nothing even to one charge, so that the governor marveled.[3]

The prophet Isaiah prophesied many years before this time that when the Messiah would come, "the government will be upon His shoulder" (Isaiah 9:6). That prophecy was still being fulfilled while Jesus was on trial by national and religious leaders. King Jesus was still in control, through His submission to His Father God, who had the first word and would have the last word about His beloved Son.

I am going to give you two more scriptural illustrations of Jesus being silent under questioning. It is so that we can more readily grasp the level of faith that operates behind the force of authority God releases us to walk in when we really totally submit to His control in all things. It's the kind of faith the Shunammite woman had in 2 Kings 4 when she said, "All is well," with a dead son lying on the bed in Elisha's guest room back home.

In Matthew 26:62–63 we read that Jesus was questioned by the high priest after witnesses testified that Jesus had said that He was able to destroy the temple of God and build it in three days. Actually, it was a misquotation of what Jesus said: "'Destroy this temple, and in three days I will raise it up'...speaking of the temple of His body" (John 2:19, 21). Jesus didn't answer a word. He left it to the Godhead to vindicate Him! And did they ever—big-time!

Luke 23:8–9 gives us the account of Jesus standing before Herod, who was hoping Jesus would do some spectacular miracle in front of him. Jesus' response to Herod's many questions was once again, "But He answered him nothing." It was distinctly refreshing to hear Mike Flynn, an Anglican priest, speak at a recent spiritual leadership conference in Southern California. He said with passion that one of the greatest needs among those who believe in allowing God to move in the power of the Holy Spirit was simply to "SHUT UP!"—meaning the great need to give God more listening time. I couldn't agree more. And I mean, as Mike did, during services. It's amazing what we would hear! But we have to be willing to be outside our comfort zones and let go of our control so that the Holy Spirit really becomes the only One in total charge! It will take a huge dose of the fear of the Lord, which is the only thing that releases us from the fear of man.

So much authority from God is dissipated by so many spiritual leaders who think they have to help God out by talking all the time. I often wonder how they will handle the shock when God commands total silence in heaven for about half an hour as described in Revelation 8:1.

Finally, when Jesus the model as the Lamb was on the cross, the meekness of His majesty was again expressed in silence when those around the cross mocked Him and challenged Him to display His power by saving Himself and coming down from the cross. Jesus responded with the same lamblike meekness in silence when challenged by

one of the robbers who was being crucified along-
side Him: "If You are the King of the Jews, save
Yourself" (Luke 23:37).

With one spoken word, Jesus had the potential
power to blast the whole mob into oblivion! His
silences through all these horrendous lies, injus-
tices, and unspeakable agonies of mind, body, soul,
and spirit are the epitome of the harnessed strength
of meekness at its zenith proportions.

Nowhere else in God's Word are we provided
with such a perfect description of our Lord Jesus as
the Lamb of God than Isaiah 53:3–9:

> He is despised and rejected by men, a Man of
> sorrows and acquainted with grief. And we
> hid, as it were, our faces from Him; He was
> despised, and we did not esteem Him.
>
> Surely He has borne our griefs and carried
> our sorrows; yet we esteemed Him stricken,
> smitten by God, and afflicted. But He was
> wounded for our transgressions, He was
> bruised for our iniquities; the chastisement
> for our peace was upon Him, and by His
> stripes we are healed.
>
> All we like sheep have gone astray; we
> have turned, every one, to his own way; and
> the LORD has laid on Him the iniquity of us
> all. He was oppressed and He was afflicted,
> yet He opened not His mouth; He was led

as a lamb to the slaughter, and as a sheep before its shearers is silent, so He opened not His mouth.

He was taken from prison and from judgment, and who will declare His generation? For He was cut off from the land of the living; for the transgressions of My people He was stricken. And they made His grave with the wicked—but with the rich at His death, because He had done no violence, nor was any deceit in His mouth.

The only appropriate response to this unequivocal display of humility and supernatural love is worship, thanksgiving, and praise. We join with the psalmist and say with intensity of conviction, "Bless the LORD, O my soul; and all that is within me, bless His holy name! Bless the LORD, O my soul, and forget not all His benefits: Who forgives all your iniquities, who heals all your diseases" (Psalm 103:1–3). "Not unto us, O LORD, not unto us, but to Your name give glory, because of Your mercy, because of Your truth" (Psalm 115:1).

How I thank God for the all too numerous times my precious Redeemer has forgiven my repented-of sins since my conversion when I was five years old—and for the many times He has healed my body because of His atoning work on the cross. My utter dependence on Him is expressed in the following old hymn:

> Not what I am, O Lord, but what You are,
> That alone can be my soul's true rest.
> Your love not mine, bids fear and doubt depart
> And calms the aching of my hurting heart,
> Your name is Love, I hear it from Your cross.
> Your name is Life, I see it in Your empty tomb.
> All lesser love is perishable dross
> But this shall light me through life's thickest
>   gloom.
> It's what I know of You, my Lord and God
> That fills my soul with peace, my life with song.
> You are my health, my joy, my staff and rod.
> Leaning on You, in weakness I am strong.[4]

JESUS' SUPREME AUTHORITY

I t is important to close this book by underlining Jesus' unquestionable authority and sovereignty. He really is in control. It is worth repeating that He is the ruling, reigning monarch of the universe. In fact, the only reason why we have breath in our bodies right now is because He is allowing it. In Job 12:10 we read, "In whose hand is the life of every living thing and the breath of all mankind."

Jesus Christ had the first word, and He will have the last word: "'I am the Alpha and the Omega, the Beginning and the End,' says the Lord, 'who is and who was and who is to come, the Almighty'" (Revelation 1:8). He has no competition. "You are worthy, O Lord, to receive glory and honor and power; for You created all things, and by Your will they exist and were created" (Revelation 4:11).

The Lord Jesus is the undefeated champion: "The LORD shall go forth like a mighty man; He shall stir up His zeal like a man of war. He shall cry out, yes, shout aloud; He shall prevail against His enemies" (Isaiah 42:13).

King David understood this concept of our God's total supremacy and absolute sovereignty when he says in Psalm 86:8–10, "Among the gods there is none like You, O Lord; nor are there any works like your works. All nations whom You have made shall come and worship before You, O Lord, and shall glorify Your name. For You are great and do wondrous things; You alone are God."

Listen to the words of Deuteronomy 32:39: "Now see that I, even I, am He, and there is no God besides Me; I kill and I make alive; I wound and I heal; nor is there any who can deliver from My hand."

More than that, the Lord Jesus Christ has an immutable, indestructible, everlasting kingdom. In Daniel 4:3 we read, "His kingdom is an everlasting kingdom, and His dominion is from generation to generation"; Daniel 6:26 says, "He is the living God, and steadfast forever; His kingdom is the one which shall not be destroyed, and His dominion shall endure to the end."

Nothing fazes Him. He's completely unflappable.

He's never on overload. He doesn't need sleep. He's the source of all energy. He described Himself to Moses as "I AM." That means He's everything—everything you and I will ever need at any time!

You may be thinking, "Well, that sure is awesome, and I believe it. But how do those facts relate to my everyday world on Planet Earth—like my difficult situation right now?" Good question. This awesome, almighty Being, King God, is not some gigantic power out in the cosmos disinterested in the affairs of the billions of creatures He created.

The Lord Jesus Christ is personally involved in and infinitely caring about the smallest details of our lives—as well as the big decisions we need to make and in our crisis times. He's listening to and answering millions of requests that come to Him simultaneously, spoken in every language and dialect on Earth, all at the same moment. He's always available and is not limited by time or space. This boggles the imagination.

We little, finite creatures of the dust cannot comprehend this omnipresent, omniscient, omnipotent God of unfathomable love, whose understanding of us is infinite (or unsearchable) according to Psalm 147:5. You may say, "Tell me how this works in the daily routine of life."

OK, let's get down to the smallest details of life to prove what I've been stating. I'm an international Bible teacher with a lot of my ministry conducted on public platforms and on television programs. I never want anything about my appearance to distract from the message I am bringing from the Lord. On a number of occasions, just before leaving for my speaking engagements, I've had difficulty in getting my baby-fine hair to do what I want it to do, so I always ask the Lord to *make* it go right. Because I know He can do anything and I know He cares, in simple childlike faith I thank Him that He will. And every time, without exception, He then takes over and makes it adjust to my need.

In Matthew 10:30 God tells us that He knows the number of the hairs on our head. That's part of His omniscience—all knowledge. I figure that it's part of His omnipotence—all powerfulness—to be able to help me to arrange those hairs on my head that will help my appearance to reflect the character of the God I'm speaking about.

Whenever I lose a pen, a comb, or keys— *anything*, small or large—I always immediately call on God to help me find them. I could fill a book with stories about answers to those prayers.

Life becomes an unending adventure of experiencing the supernatural intervention of the Creator of the universe in my mundane circumstances. As I have stated earlier in this book, prayer is bringing God into every situation and asking Him to change it from something natural into something supernatural so that He can get all the glory.

Here's another story that was told me personally, recently, by the wife of the Iranian family that
we are helping to disciple for the Lord Jesus. Mary's
husband, Carmi, had given her $2,500 toward the
payments of their monthly bills. When she went to
put the money in the bank, to her absolute amazement and dismay, she couldn't find it. For the next
three days she searched her home with the utmost
diligence. Then Carmi and Mary, separately, asked
God to show them what had happened to it. On the
third day, while at Mary's place of employment, she
was asking God's help about the lost money when
she heard the Holy Spirit speaking quietly into her
spirit these words. "Look for the money among
your shoes."

The moment she returned home, she made a
beeline for the shoes in her closet, and sure enough,
there was the exact amount of $2,500 sitting in a
pair of her shoes! Mary said she hasn't a clue how
in the world the money could have gotten there. But
one thing she does know. God is amazingly real,
and in His infinite knowledge and caring concern
for her, His child, He communicated clearly into
her mind what to do to meet her need—when she
asked in faith and trust. That's a God incident, not
a coincidence!

I love to think about how God is described
in Deuteronomy 33:26: "There is none like
God...who rides through the heavens to your

help, and in his majesty through the skies" (RSV).
Wow, what a God!

This would be an appropriate place to stop and
sing the following praise song to Him:

> We declare Your majesty
> We proclaim that Your name is exalted
> For You reign magnificently
> Rule victoriously
> Your power is shown throughout the earth
> Lift up Your name, for You are holy
> Sing it again, all honor and glory
> In adoration we bow before Your throne.[1]

Why don't you invite God to take complete
control of your life? Sell out to Him. Ask the Lord
Jesus to forgive you for your sins. Thank Him for
taking the punishment and penalty of them when
He died on the cross for you. Invite Him to come
and live within your heart, and believe and thank
Him that He will on the basis of John 1:12: "As
many as received Him, to them He gave the right
to become children of God, to those who believe in
His name."

Believe me, and millions like me, who can
testify that we do ourselves the greatest favor by
living our lives in total submission to the lordship
of Jesus Christ. It's the greatest adventure known
to man. There's no greater spiritual ambition than

to want to know and understand God's character and ways in order to make Him, and them, known to others in the power of the Holy Spirit. We must also invite and allow the Holy Spirit to change us and to conform us into the likeness of our magnificent Master, the beautiful Lord Jesus Christ. It's the only pathway to fulfillment. All else is frustration. Will you pursue these goals with me? I'm praying fervently that you will, dear reader.

O TO BE LIKE THEE

O to be like Thee, blessed Redeemer,
This is my constant longing and prayer;
Gladly I'll forfeit all of earth's treasures,
Jesus, Thy perfect likeness to wear.

O to be like Thee, O to be like Thee,
Blessed Redeemer, pure as Thou art;
Come in Thy sweetness, come in Thy fullness;
Stamp Thine own image deep on my heart.

O to be like Thee, full of compassion,
Loving, forgiving, tender and kind,
Helping the helpless, cheering the fainting,
Seeking the wand'ring sinner to find.

O to be like Thee, Lord, I am coming,
Now to receive th' anointing divine,

All that I am and have I am bringing,
Lord, from this moment all shall be Thine.

O to be like Thee, while I am pleading,
Pour out Thy Spirit, fill with Thy love,
Make me a temple meet for Thy dwelling,
Fit me for life and Heaven above.[2]

TO BE LIKE JESUS

To be like Jesus, to be like Jesus,
All I ask is to be like Him,
All through life's journey, from earth to glory,
All I ask is to be like Him.[3]

Notes

Chapter 1
Jesus the Model in Ministry

1. Johnston M. Cheney, *The Life of Christ in Stereo* (Sisters, OR: Multnomah, 1984).

Chapter 3
Jesus Was Forthright and Transparently Open

1. Cheney, *The Life of Christ in Stereo.*

Chapter 6
Jesus the Master Soulwinner

1. "Make Me a Winner of Souls" by John W. Peterson. Copyright © 1953 by John W. Peterson Music Company. All rights reserved. Used by permission.

Chapter 8
Jesus the Model as the Lamb

1. "For All My Sin" by Norman J. Clayton. Copyright © 1943, renewed 1971 Wordspring Music, LLC (admin. by Word Music Group, Inc.). All rights reserved. Used by permission.

2. "O to Be Like Thee" by Thomas O. Chisholm. Public domain.

3. Cheney, *The Life of Christ in Stereo.*

4. Title and author unknown.

CHAPTER 9
JESUS' SUPREME AUTHORITY

1. "We Declare Your Majesty" by Malcolm Du Plessis, copyright © 1984 Maranatha Praise, Inc. (admin. by Music Services). All rights reserved. Used by permission.

2. "O to Be Like Thee" by Thomas O. Chisholm. Public domain.

3. "To Be Like Jesus" by L. C. Hall. Public domain.

HEAR JOY DAWSON TEACH ON ALMOST 200 DIFFERENT KEY SUBJECTS—

IDEAL FOR TRAINING SCHOOLS, BIBLE INSTITUTES, CHURCHES, HOME GROUPS, OR PRIVATE STUDY.

For your free Resource Guide, contact:

LOS ANGELES YOUTH WITH A MISSION
11141 Osborne Street
Lake View Terrace, CA 91342
Phone: 818.896.2755
Fax: 818.897.6738
E-mail: info@ywamla.org
Web site: www.ywamla.org

OTHER TITLES BY JOY DAWSON

The Fire of God
This enlightening, challenging, and encouraging book explains how we can come through the inevitable heat of life's circumstances, more like Jesus, but unscarred by the flames.

Forever Ruined for the Ordinary
This exciting book explains how to experience the adventure of hearing and obeying God's voice as a way of life.

Intercession, Thrilling and Fulfilling
This inspiring manual takes the reader to greater depths and breadth in effective prayer for others.

Intimate Friendship With God
This insightful best seller explains how God's standards of holiness affect every area of our lives.

Some of the Ways of God in Healing
If you have more questions than answers about healing, then this book is for you. Joy is ruthless in her pursuit of truth from God's Word.

Influencing Children to Become World Changers
Filled with wisdom, inspiration, and fascinating real-life stories, this practical book is a must-read

for everyone who desires to impact children to enable them to reach their God-ordained destinies and help shape the world.

To order these titles or to obtain your free Resource Guide of Joy Dawson's teaching materials, contact:

LOS ANGELES YOUTH WITH A MISSION
11141 Osborne Street
Lake View Terrace, CA 91342
Phone: 818.896.2755
Fax: 818.897.6738
E-mail: info@ywamla.org
Web site: www.ywamla.org

Witchcraft in the
Pews

George
Bloomer